THRESHERS
at Work

Hans Halberstadt

Motorbooks International
Publishers & Wholesalers ®

Dedication
For Jacob and Anna Yoder, and their family, with thanks.

ACKNOWLEDGMENTS
Thanks to: C. H. Wendel, Orrin Iseminger, Dale Hartley, John Richmond, the Ardenwood Historic Farm threshing crew, Terry Kubicek, Paul Bazetta, the Yoder family, Donald Swenson, Bob Blades, Stan Mayberry, Cecil Monson, and Dave Erb, all of whom helped one way or another.

A special thanks to the Case company for their generous and friendly support of projects like this one, and the tremendous help from people like Dave Rogers and Eldon Brumbaugh.

First published in 1995 by Motorbooks International Publishers & Wholesalers, 729 Prospect Avenue, PO Box 1, Osceola, WI 54020-0001

Motorbooks International books are also available at discounts in bulk quantity for industrial or sales-promotional use. For details write to Special Sales Manager at the Publisher's address

Library of Congress Cataloging-in-Publication Data Available
ISBN 0-7603-0133-6

On the front cover: George Cabral drives a pair of his beautiful, matched black Percherons hitched to a still-functional McCormick-Deering grain harvester. Those sweeps just miss George's head as they slowly revolve, raking the cut grain from the platform.

On the title page: Too much air coming from the cleaning fan causes a lot of grain to build up in the straw pile. Such problems are common at the beginning of a "set," and adjustments on the machine will quickly fix the problem.

On the back cover: The Yoder family collect bundles of oats from their field. Young Lewis Yoder, who is just learning to drive, is at the controls.

Printed in Hong Kong

CONTENTS

THRESHING TIME

Jacob and Merlin Yoder, father and son, hitch the three big Belgian horses at the door of the old barn across the lane from the house, early on a warm, dry Ohio June morning. They farm 80 acres in eastern Ohio, three generations on a little farm, off a little gravel road, in a quiet corner of America that hasn't really changed much in 100 years, or maybe more.

The horses stand patiently, the way Belgians do, while Jacob fits the hames, the collars, crupper, belly-band, breeching, all the straps and buckles. Jacob hitches up inside the barn, beneath hand-hewn logs that probably grew on this old farm, long ago. There are stalls for six horses, and all are in residence—four Belgian "drafters" and a pair of sleek thoroughbred carriage horses that pull the buggy to town or for visits to neighbors.

All the horses get at least a quart of grain every day, more when they work hard, to augment the feed supplied by hay and pasture. That grain is typically oats, and the Yoders grow it themselves. Ten acres on a good year will supply the fuel for these horses for a year, at minimal out-of-pocket cost.

Jacob takes the reins, clucks to the team, and walks them to the waiting wagon. He

Jacob may honor traditional ways, but he takes care of his horses, too; that's why he's attached this gasoline engine to power the old binder, taking much of the load off the team.

The Yoders thresh right in the barn, with the grain going directly to the bin and the straw right into the barn. Their threshing machine is a Dion, a Canadian brand, and the last company to build threshers in North America.

Oats, harvested with a horse-drawn binder, stand in the field waiting to be threshed in Holmes County, Ohio.

backs them into position, clips the eveners to the harness, then tosses the lines up on the box of the wagon where little Lewis Yoder, age 8, waits and attentively watches his grandfather. Lewis is learning to drive, and like any farm boy, is excited and apprehensive about this new skill and responsibility.

Jacob climbs aboard, followed by Lewis' father, Merlin. The team moves off with the empty wagon, through the gate and up the hill to the field where the bundles of oats stand in orderly clusters of sheaves.

Jacob drives the wagon into position on the right side of the first row of bundles; Merlin clambers down, pitchfork in hand, and begins tossing the bundles up into the wagon. He is an artist at it, each bundle of oats delivered with the grain heads inboard, the butts out, in an orderly row. Jacob

8

Amish farmers still rely on the binder to cut grain, as this man is doing near Kidron, Ohio. The binder was one of the essential tools for the revolution that transformed the American farm from a subsistence operation to a profitable business back in the late 1800s.

makes minor adjustments while young Lewis minds the team.

The first shock is cleaned from the field, the horses lean into their collars and position the wagon alongside the next in the row. Within a few minutes the wagon is full to near overflowing, with Jacob and Lewis perched high up on the load. Lewis watches the team, reins in hand, ready for any tricky behavior from the team while his father and grandfather work. Then the team is ordered into motion again. Leaning back against the breeching to hold the loaded wagon on the hillside, they bring the oats back to the old barn, where the Dion threshing machine is ready for duty. It is threshing day for another year on the American family farm.

The Legend And Lore of Threshing

This little pageant was once a common event on almost every farm in America and Canada. Today you will see it at old time farm shows and threshing bees, a kind of amateur act and "living history" performance. But for the Yoders and their Ohio Amish neighbors, threshing machines still clean the grain, pretty much the same way as has been done since the time of the Civil War. More modern farmers have nearly all converted to combines.

Threshing day is payday for grain farmers. It was, and still is, a single day on most farms. And it was, and still is, a tremendously special day—a kind of working party for the farmer and his family.

Seventy years ago, across the heartland, all your neighbors would show up to help bring in the crop. It took at least a dozen men and boys, a big steam engine, and a sturdy, reliable "thrashing" machine to clean the grain. But that team could (if they knew their business, if the crop was good, the machinery was big enough, and nothing broke) thresh 2,000 bushels of grain or more in a single day. It was done with shared machines, shared labor, and a shared sense of community.

Back then, and in a few places yet today, neighbors formed "threshing rings" for this ritual event. The threshing machine, and the steam engine or gasoline tractor that powered it, might be owned by one farmer or purchased by members of the ring.

So why did all these farmers—a notoriously independent breed—cooperate so well? For one thing, it was a way of trading labor. Most farms didn't need a lot of manpower, except at threshing time,

Tom Coles learned about horses and binders after a career in business, but he is now a stalwart volunteer at Ardenwood Historic Farm, on the shores of San Francisco Bay. Ardenwood is one of many places in the U.S. and Canada where you can enjoy watching—and helping with—the harvest chores of the traditional farm.

This is Jacob Yoder, cutting oats. As Orrin Iseminger says of the process, "The binder makes music. A beautifully shocked field makes art. Cutting, shocking, and threshing make poetry. But it is hot, sweaty, doggone hard work."

Jacob takes the lines while young Lewis carefully studies the proceedings. The oats they harvest will feed those horses through the year—horse "fuel" the family can produce itself, essentially for free. That kind of economy was once treasured on the American farm, and still is within the Amish community.

and a threshing ring was a formal way of guaranteeing enough help at harvest time.

There was another reason, too, and one fondly remembered by many men today. That was the noon meal, the legendary "threshing dinner" that was, as one old-timer reported, ". . . like Thanksgiving dinner every day." Farm wives didn't cooperate with their neighbors at harvest time, they competed with their friends down the road for the reputation of 'Best Cook.'

Those farm women would plot and scheme and get up at 3:00 in the morning to get the roasts and the pies in the oven; the chickens killed, plucked and fried; the potatoes peeled, boiled and mashed.

They'd cook until noon, with the help of all the girls in the family and anybody they could hire from town, then serve it and watch it all disappear. Clean up might last till midnight. Like so many other things within the American family farm tradition, the motivation involved a sense of honor, duty, and responsibility, more than money.

The Yoders were part of a threshing ring until quite recently, but now thresh by themselves. They, and their Amish neighbors, all have threshers of their own, small Canadian Dions, usually suitable for the few acres of grain each family typically grows.

Jacob and Merlin have their thresher set up just inside the barn. The cleaned grain will be blown directly

With young Lewis at the controls, the Yoders collect the bundles of oats from their field.

into the grain bin. The bins are directly over the horses' stalls, a very convenient arrangement at feeding time. Although most Amish won't use a tractor for plowing or planting, lots of Amish farmers own and use tractors for stationary power needs, particularly for running a thresher. The Yoders have a Massey Ferguson, neatly belted up to the thresher and ready to go.

Jacob drives the team up the ramp, into the barn. The horses stop on command, the wagon neatly positioned alongside the thresher's feeder. Merlin starts the tractor, engages the clutch gradually, then brings the engine speed up to operating speed. The old Dion whirrs along in a business-like way, ready for action.

Up on the bundle wagon, Merlin puts on a dust mask, then starts to feed the machine. One bundle after another is forked from the neat rows on the wagon, then plops onto the feeder and is quickly gobbled up. The bundles land on the feeder in a smooth, steady stream—head first, without gaps. Merlin makes it look easy.

The barn fills with dust from the oat chaff. A stream of clean grain flows like water into the grain bin while a pile of straw builds quickly in the loft. The horses stand patiently, despite the noise and fog of chaff. Jacob clambers up on the wagon to help and in a few minutes the bundles have all been run through the Dion and it is time to go back for another load. After a half dozen cycles of this routine, the field is clean and the job is done. In one afternoon the Yoders have filled the grain bins that will help feed the horses for a year.

George Cabral has spent a lot of his lifetime looking at the southern end of a northbound horse. Here are six of his handsome, matched Percherons hitched to a "header" harvester—one of the very last still in working condition anywhere in North America.

Here comes George Cabral and a sight that has almost vanished from American and Canadian agriculture—a header harvester in action. That wagon isn't warped, it was built that way for just this job; It is called a "header wagon," and this one goes back to before World War 1. Once the wagon is full, the loose material is delivered to the thresher and forked into the feeder.

Threshing Memories

As a thresher, my grandfather Charles Kubicek ran a Nichols and Shepard Steam Traction Engine in co-ownership with his brother Fredrick. A large round stock tank for water, a water wagon with hand pump, two wagon racks for carrying bundles and the threshing machine rounded out his equipment list. Many folks also called the threshing machine a separator as it did separate the wheat from the chaff.

Threshing, or better known by Czech and German farmers as "thrashing" in Saline County, Nebraska was a tough, long day or days, or even weeks of work. The crews were usually made up of farm neighbors and relatives, and well acquainted with the work and their appointed jobs.

Grandfather liked to run eight racks, which meant eight drivers, at least two spike pitchers in the field (they pitched from the ground up and into the rack), two rack pitchers, a thresher boss on the threshing machine, the steam engineer, a water boy on the water wagon to provide water for the steam engine boiler and at least one dog to watch everybody. With eight racks working, two racks would be unloading at the separator, two racks would be in the field loading bundles, two racks would be coming from the field and two racks returning to the field. Horses pulled the racks and could be skittish around a steam engine.

Charlie Kubicek often took his two sons Lumir and George to thresh, if the job was close to the family farm. My father, Lumir, remembered that during the thirties, on a particularly windy, dusty, humid, hot iron on your head sort of day, the rack pitchers decided to choke the thresher and thereby get a rest until the separator was once again ready. The usual method on a smaller machine was to pitch two or three bundles together and sideways. If the thresher could not handle the load, the flywheels would stop and the main belt would be thrown off. It might take

20 minutes to an hour to open the thresher, find the slug, pull the straw out, adjust the belts and reset the steam engine. It gave a rest to the crew as they watched the thresher boss and the engineer clear the thresher and reset the equipment.

On the particular day, as remembered by my father Lumir, the rack pitchers decided to really test the big 32-64 Baker machine. Five bundles went into the feeder at once and cross wise. Grandfather watched the engine closely and the thresher even more closely. He saw the bundles hit the feeder in a tangled bunch. Knowing that there was a second or two of lag time from the moment the bundle hit the feeder until it reached the cylinder, grandfather grabbed the rope tied to the sawyers handle on the governor and opened the steam flow wide open. The threshing machine by then had just started to lug down, but the brute strength of the added steam flow powered through the slug and the wind-stacker roared as the folly of the rack pitchers cleared the machine. The remnants of the bundles were blown onto the straw pile like so many others before them. The thresher boss by now knew what had happened and was mad as hell. Dad remembered they got a cussing out and threatened with reassignment as spike pitchers in the field. There was no more nonsense for the rest of the day. Grandfather always spoke admiringly of that Baker machine. He must of worn it out because by the late thirties or early forties he had a Case 22-37 threshing machine, which is still stored in the machine shed along with the Sandwich 8 hole corn-sheller. The Nichols and Shepard 20-70 Steam Engine survived the dirty thirties, the war forties and into the early nifty fifties. And then for $50.00 was cut-up for scrap. The steam whistle, however, survives on my own Nichols and Shepard 20-70 Steam Traction Engine.

It has its own signature sound and I hope it is a comfort to the souls of my great grandfather, grandfather, and father. They are at rest together in the nearby Riverside Cemetery. They all ran steam, threshed wheat and oats, shelled corn and survived. They created a family tradition of hard work, built a foundation for the next generation, and were a part of the bigger legacy of American Agriculture.

Grandfather also remembered that the last meal, whether supper or dinner, was always accompanied by a glass of beer. The threshing crew then finished and moved on. Even during the days of prohibition, the Czech and German families honored the custom. Beer was home brewed, stored in the cellar and served for special occasions. Finishing the harvest on a given farm was just such a special occasion.

Of course, all the women competed to serve meals and lunches of the best meats; potatoes; corn on the cob; vegetables from the garden; bread baked the night before; kolache pastries with prune, poppy seed, apricot, peach or cherry filling; and of course gallons of coffee—strong, with milk and with sugar. Everyone ate like a draft horse and worked like a draft horse.

When dinner was served at noon, the crews usually went to the house to eat. Extra tables would be set, but if room inside was not available, then tables under the trees and in the shade would be set. A wash stand was usually set up outside with towels. Washing up involved an outside wash stand for two or three men at a time with strong homemade lye soap, lots of hot wash water and lots and lots of cold rinse water for the hands, the forearms, the neck, and of course the head. Towel off the water, run a comb or hands through your hair and you were ready to eat.

After dinner, the crews would rest a bit; the engineer would stoke the firebox, refill the boiler with water and check the fuel and water bunkers. A good engineer would also recheck the oilers, and the journals, tighten anything that was loose and get ready to go again. The horses were fed and watered, harness checked and hooves inspected. When all was ready, a short whistle and the choreographed process began again.

—Terry Kubicek
Saline County, Nebraska

"Yes, the binder was complicated,
but it was fascinating to see it work.
I never got tired of watching it,
even after cutting thousands of acres of
grain with one while I was a kid.
I drove the A-C "C" that pulled the
old Deering binder equipped with a
Carlson Drive PTO conversion.
Grandpa, 75, rode the binder.
He ran the bundle rack,
adjusted the height of cut,
and hollered at me whenever
I steered crooked.

"The binder made music.
A beautifully shocked field made art.
Cutting, shocking, and threshing was
poetry. But, it was hot, sweaty, scratchy,
doggone hard work."

—Orrin Iseminger

The threshing machine, or separator, was in business long before the practical binder came along in the 1880s. From the 1840s to around 1900 you could find harvesters like this one cutting grain and leaving it loose on the ground. George Cabral drives a pair of his beautiful matched black Percherons hitched to a still-functional McCormick-Deering grain harvester. Those sweeps just miss George's head as they slowly revolve, raking the cut grain from the platform.

A gaggle of ancient threshers on display at Rollag, Minnesota. Rollag hosts one of the largest congregations of steam engines every year, over the first weekend in September, and threshing demonstrations are always part of the program.

Detail, Case thresher.

Merlin Yoder tosses bundles onto the Dion's feeder. Merlin makes it look easy, but there is an art to it—one bundle follows the next, without gaps, and always with the heads going in first.

Ready for the first bundles, the Dion whirs as the power is applied to the belt. The Yoder's barn is an old one, with hand-hewn beams and mortise-and-tennon joinery.

A late-model, all-steel Advance-Rumley thresher gets inspected prior to action at the annual Camp Creek show at Waverly, Nebraska.

The team on the bundle wagon, a pair of sturdy
Belgians, doesn't seem to mind the noise and the clatter
and the whirring belts nearby. You certainly can't do this
with all horses, but Belgians and the other sturdy breeds
favored by American farmers quickly learn what's
expected of them and a good horse will do what he can
to help out.

John Tower's Advance steamer is still getting a workout,
just as it was designed to do, powering a McCormick-
Deering thresher. Although John trots the steamer out
for shows occasionally, he also fires it up to work on his
family's old homestead, near Copperopolis in the
foothills of the Sierra Nevada.

21

First-hand Account

My parents were farmers in southern Minnesota all their lives on a farm just west of LeRoy until Dad retired in the early 1960s and moved to town. We belonged to a threshing ring until around 1950, which was about when I left the farm for good also. There were generally about 12 of us in the ring every year.

The threshing machine and the 30-60 Aultman Taylor were owned by one of the farmers. The farmer moved the rig from farm to farm and charged according to what he threshed for each farmer based on the dump counter. His job was to keep the machine running, maintain it, set it up at each farm and make sure as little grain was lost as possible. I'm not sure any more what kind of machine he had, but it was large.

When two of us young guys were pitching bundles into it we would try to plug it just for fun. The tractor operator would hear the 30-60 snort and would run for the throttle. I can still hear him yell while he was on his way. We were never able to plug the threshing machine and never got in trouble for trying as long as we didn't throw bundles in crossways. I suspect he knew who was going to try this stuff on him and stayed a little closer when we were up.

It was an art running a bundle team. The horses got so they knew when and where to stop when you were in the field loading up so you didn't have to pay much attention to them. How you loaded the rack made a lot of difference when you were unloading, so I was always very careful how I put the bundles on the wagon.

All of us took a lot of pride in our nice full loads with high, straight sides and loaded mostly high enough so you had to worry some about tipping. And yes, we had tractors we could have used to pull the wagons with, but it took two men where one could do it with horses. My team was a pair of 1900-pound Belgians that I would dearly love to have here on the place today. They didn't like being on the side of the apron the belt was on so I always tried to get them on the other side. You were expected to take turns on the belt side, so it didn't always work out.

We dug holes for the machine both to set and keep it level and to keep it in place when the belt was tensioned. We took the tongue off the machine and slid it under the front. The belt was very long both so it wouldn't slip under load and so we could get up to the apron of the machine easily. The belt was always run straight because that's the way the pulleys had to turn. The only reason for twisting a belt was to get proper direction on the drive pulley.

And we always took the belts off at night. The 30-60 Aultman-Taylor was both a delight and a pain in the neck. It was slow on the road and seemed to take forever to move from one farm to the next.

It had chain and drum steering so the operator was always spinning the steering wheel from one side to the other to keep it going straight down the road. It was very difficult to get into a lot of farm driveways because it turned so slowly and the driveways were mostly very narrow. It was a joy on the belt—smooth and steady with lots of reserve power. The steam guys can say what they want about their engines, but I would put that Aultman-Taylor up against any of them. I'll bet the best part of threshing everywhere was those meals at noon.

We would go run a bundle team all day in the heat and sun and never complain at all just so we could eat the food. It was great being around the neighbors too and those of us in the younger single group had a lot of fun horsing around. It didn't hurt anything and turned something that was an awful lot of hard work into play for a lot of us. I wish every one of you who really likes old tractors and machinery could spend just one of those days on that threshing rig.

—Cecil E. Monson
Mountainville, NY

Threshing machines are alive and well at dozens or even hundreds of farm shows across Canada and the U.S. This one happens to be at Hamilton, Missouri, a small, delightful show where the crowds are local folks and friendly neighbors.

It's a nasty job, but somebody has to do it. Happily, not us! Even with the "wind-stacker" to help manage the straw pile, the threshermen at the end of the machine have a hot, dirty assignment.

CHAPTER 2

THE HISTORY OF THRESHING

No matter what anybody tells you, the good old days were *rotten*—at least the old days on the farms of 200 years ago—particularly on grain farms. It took a full day of sweaty, back-breaking work to plow one acre of ground, and plow it rather poorly at that. Seeding was done by hand, much of it becoming bird feed in short order. Yields were small, on small fields. Harvest was done with a single-handed sickle, the ripe grain held in one hand, the bunch cut with the knife in the other. The work of the "reapers" was slow, brutal labor.

Cutting grain was man's work but gathering up the gavels and tying the grain into bundles was done by the women of the family, the "bandsters." These bundles or sheaves of harvested grain were then carried off to the barn or granary for threshing. In the old days, threshing was winter work, done indoors. Until about 1830 in the U.S. and Canada (and still today in some parts of the world) the straw was spread on the floor in a layer about a foot deep, then threshed with flails or trod with oxen or horses.

Historic farms like Ardenwood in Fremont California conduct threshing and harvest demonstrations all over the U.S. and Canada. The Ardenwood crew will put 1,000 bundles through this machine over the course of a weekend, with plenty of help from visitors.

This huge Yellow Boy thresher is one of the biggest ever, with a 42-inch cylinder and 70-inch separator. While many wooden threshers were built over the years, few survive.

A flail is a stick or pole about six feet long, attached to another, shorter section of flat wood, the beater. The hinge is typically leather. The threshers walk slowly around the pile of straw, literally beating the grain from it with these simple clubs.

Threshing grain this way was notoriously difficult, tiring work that exhausted and even killed people engaged in the labor over a period of weeks. It was also notorious for producing bumps and bruises on the thresher's head, arms, and upper torso until the thresher learned to give the flail a little twist on the up-stroke.

The only real alternative to the flail was using oxen or other livestock to walk across the straw, their hooves breaking open the heads of grain. Now, this system is a lot easier on the thresher, but has a major drawback—the sanitary habits of livestock are notoriously poor. Having all that livestock "exhaust" mixed in with the grain, was not considered desirable even back then. But that was the way it was done, back in the "not-so-good-old-days."

The Industrial Revolution

While many people think the computer revolution has been the major transformation of modern times, current changes are nothing compared to what was happening in America 150 years ago. It was a

Steam powered most threshers over the years, and many old members of the American Brotherhood of Threshermen will still maintain that steam tractors were far superior to gasoline for the job.

Case manufactured more threshing machines than any other company and dominated the industry right up until 1953 when the last one was built. This all-steel model is one of the last, and it remains in excellent and functional condition, ready for work at Hamilton, Missouri.

time when anybody and everybody could be a scientist and an inventor—an era of free-lance engineering and discovery. The steam engine, the railroad, the telegraph, the photograph, the steamboat, and many other extremely important inventions came on the scene within a few years of each other, a couple of decades before 1850. All sorts of uneducated people successfully tinkered together new devices for solving old problems. That extraordinary tinkering has been immortalized in the expression "Yankee ingenuity," a salute to the innovation and spirit of the American technical creativity. And Yankee ingenuity was especially demonstrated in the many machines and devices designed to serve American agriculture.

American farmers brought most of their agricultural technology and practices with them from the old country—Europe. Reapers, powered fanning mills and steam-powered threshers of various sorts

This old Case thresher has spent most of its life under cover and remains ready for action. That's the exception, not the rule for threshers; they tend to be left out in a corner of the lower 40, rusting quickly into oblivion.

A Russell steam engine stands by for the signal to apply power to the belt. This rig is served by an ancient pickup truck—too small a load to keep the thresher fed for long. A standard bundle wagon would be slower, but haul about ten times the volume of shocks.

had been in common use in England during the later part of the eighteenth century. And the American colonists, especially the wealthy ones, sent home for all sorts of machines. It is supposed that Bell's reaper and Meikle's thresher were imported to America before the end of the 18th century.

But remember, by the time of the American Revolution in 1776, the colonists were not getting along too well with the Old Country. Shipments of all sorts of important items halted and then stopped completely. The war for American independence was not just the beginning of political independence. It was going to be the beginning of technological autonomy as well.

Fortunately, America had both the mechanics and the natural resources to design and build its own machinery. *The Grain Harvesters,* a history of agriculture written by historians Graeme Quick and Wesley Buchele, reports that the first threshing machine patent in America was awarded to Samuel Mulliken of Philadelphia in 1791. Yankee ingenuity was off and running.

Looking at the types and numbers of patents that were filed, it's amazing to see how quick and clever these Yankees actually were. As soon as one fellow patented a mower or reaper or thresher, someone else borrowed his idea and modified it. Then they sent an application along to the patent office, hoping to cash in on the idea. News of successful innovations and inventions traveled quickly. While we usually think of early American farmers as isolated, rural and conservative, many farmers read various agricultural newspapers and were interested in experimenting with new farming practices.

Those early agricultural handbooks and newspapers were imported from England. After the Revolutionary War and especially after the War of 1812, the

29

The left side of Donald Swensen's 1948 Red River Special. The large belt drives the blower. This machine was lovingly restored by the Swensen family over the course of many months. It is one of the star performers at Rollag, Minnesota, every year.

European sources were cut off and American agricultural news came from Philadelphia and New York. Both cities had active, organized agricultural societies that printed papers and circulated news of new farming developments. And ingenious Yankees were never reluctant to borrow and modify any idea that would lighten their work . . . or make them some money.

The Pressures of Competition

Looking back over a century and a half of agricultural technological development, it's easy to pick out the leaders; J.I. Case gets the credit for the thresher, Cyrus McCormick takes the honors for the reaper and John Deere is remembered today for important improvements to the plow. We sometimes

Another look at the Swensen family's Red River Special, a 22-foot by 36-foot model. While careful restorations of tractors are common, such attention to a thresher is rare. Most of the work was accomplished by Eric Swensen as a project for his high school shop class. The thresher was found in a junk yard near Star Lake, Minnesota. The wood was rotten and the sheet metal was pretty well rusted away, but it performs like new at the Western Minnesota Steam Thresher's Reunion at Rollag every Labor Day weekend.

tend to overlook all the important competition in each field, the dozens of other inventors and companies that each made important contributions to the evolution of a particular machine.

The reaper was invented in the 1830s. We generally tip our hat to Cyrus McCormick for the patent honors, but several people came up with workable machines about the same time. The famous lawsuit between John Manny and Cyrus McCormick was filed in 1854 and was not finally settled until 1861. There was a tremendous amount of patent litigation

even before the Civil War, and some extremely creative inventors ended up dying in poverty, while waiting for the legal recognition and financial benefits of their contributions.

John Deere's plow was developed about the same time, making cultivation faster and easier—allowing the difficult prairie sod to be broken for the first time. But Deere owed his start to Leonard Andrus and the Grand Detour Plow Company, another historic and venerable name in farm implements. And the Oliver Chilled Plow Works, founded

Big combines like this one started to replace threshers in the West very early, back in the 1860s and 1970s. This one is a Harris Harvester, a 1918 model, and it still works just fine. Cliff Koster's father bought it new, and it still resides in the barn where it has always been stored.

in 1855, certainly provided additional competition for John Deere, and innovation in the plow business for the American farmer.

J. I. Case also had some important competition but was able to build a significant market for his machinery by going west to the prairies. A fairly effi-

cient thresher was built by the Albany Agricultural Works in New York, Emery and Company, Proprietors, as early as 1853. But unless a farmer lived fairly close to the Erie Canal or a railroad line, it was difficult to have a thresher delivered.

Along with the Reaper

A few somewhat crude, but highly effective inventions helped farmers thresh grain before an actual thresher was available. There were:

The Hedgehog

A simple, but effective threshing device, called a "hedgehog," came along just about the same time as the reaper, from an unknown inventor. No more than a section of log with pegs sticking out, and spinning on an axle, the hedgehog did a fast, pretty effective job of knocking the kernels of grain out of the heads. Most were hand-cranked, but some were powered by horses or falling water. The hedgehog was simple enough for the local blacksmith to build, once he had the idea, and effective enough that farmers clamored for them.

Threshing with a hedgehog was far faster, easier, and cleaner than previous methods of knocking the grain out of the heads. Basically, one person turned the crank while another inserted a handful of cut grain into the spinning pegs—holding onto the straw and keeping fingers out of the way. Those pegs quickly broke the kernels loose, allowing them to drop into a container below the machine. When the grain was threshed, the straw was discarded into a pile.

The Fanning Mill

Along with the kernels of wheat, barley, or oats, was a considerable percentage of chaff and straw fragments. The traditional way to get rid of this material was to pour it from an elevated platform—the top of the barn, perhaps—on a breezy day; the lighter chaff to be carried away while the small, dense kernels dropping onto a big tray or tarp.

Naturally, people improvised fans to help with this process over the years, and Graeme Quick and Wesley Buchele's excellent book, *The Grain Harvesters*, describes Chinese fanning mills built as far back as the 14th century. But during the early years of the Industrial Revolution simple mechanized fans were invented, fabricated, and put to work in large numbers—inspired by imported Chinese ideas or developed spontaneously, we don't now know. But by 1800 such devices were quite common and fairly sophisticated.

Although necessity may be the mother of invention, the title of godmother probably belongs to repetitious drudgery. And it is repetitious drudgery that should also get the credit for producing divine inspiration. The history books are full of inspired luminaries like Hugh V. McKay, Jerome I. Case, Henry Ford and scores of others. Their own endurance of back-breaking farm drudgery provided the personal incentive to design agricultural machinery that would eventually replace the primitive fanning mills and "hedgehogs" and make the work easier.

This crew attends a little McCormick-Deering 26-inch thresher at Silver Bend, California. McCormick-Deering was, along with Case, one of the leading builders of threshers.

This contented gent is Stan Mayberry, and you can't blame him for feeling smug. That's because he commands this handsome 1919 Advance steam engine, chuffing away at 250rpm, and he's got a big Case thresher under power on the other end of that belt. He bought this machine when he was just 15 years old, brought it back to life, and puts it to work in the Northern Missouri area around Hamilton.

More About That Ingenious Yankee, Jerome I. Case

Jerome Increase Case was not the first inventor of the thresher, nor the second, nor even the third. But he was the pioneer of the production of threshing machines and was a major force in opening the Midwest up to large scale farming. And the story of his career in threshing not only illustrates the history of American threshing technology, it also seems to reflect the typical pattern of technological development and growth in American society. He is credited with eventually becoming the largest and earliest manufacturer of threshers, pioneering the industry and helping to open the prairie to farming.

Jerome got his start in threshing from his father, Caleb Case, a New York farmer who was also a thresherman. Reading *The Genessee Farmer*, a New York farm periodical in the 1830's, Caleb noticed an article about the Groundhog thresher. He bought one, eventually becoming one of the earliest thresher dealers in America. And he put his four sons to work, operating a custom threshing business for his neighbors.

We know that by the late 1830s and the 1840s, the construction and operation of threshing machines of various types was already a mature industry in America. Hundreds of laborers were already in the threshing business, either as farmers or as hired hands, operating a thresher. Some threshing operations used water power if it was available, others used horses. But it was still a very labor intensive chore, a dusty, dirty operation that took a lot of time, even when you were fortunate enough to have a power source of some sort.

Young J. I. Case had the opportunity to attend Rensselear Institute in New York during his teenage

Right side view, McCormick-Deering 26-foot thresher with extended feeder and wind stacker.

years. After this short stint of technical training he returned to work as a custom thresherman, working in his father's business. At age 22 he went west, down the Erie canal and across Lake Michigan to Wisconsin. Historians David Erb and Eldon Brumbaugh describe Case's early beginnings in their comprehensive biography of the Case corporation, *Full Steam Ahead*.

Case took six Groundhog threshers with him, probably acquired from his father's inventory. J. I. Case demonstrated and sold the machines as he went, saving one to set himself up in the custom threshing business in Wisconsin.

Settling in Rochester, Wisconsin, Jerome I. Case rented a shop to make repairs and modifications to his thresher. He had seen the possibility of improving on the machine and he wanted to combine the threshing and cleaning operations. Experimenting with the design, he consulted a local fanning mill operator named Richard Ely. After two years of designing, building and trying various prototypes, Case finally had a machine that would perform to his satisfaction. First demonstrated in 1844, the machine operated successfully and was quickly put into production.

Case located his first thresher factory in Racine, Wisconsin and built six harvesters the first year. They sold quickly. He built more, but soon demand exceeded his production capability. Although no accurate construction drawings of these first production machines exist, it is believed that the first threshers were small, horse powered machines.

We do however, have pictures and a complete description from advertising posters a few years later, printed about 1848. The Case Thresher is described as an improved Wemple machine with the Pitt's Patent separator. Remember that one of the hallmarks of Yankee ingenuity is to use and adapt existing technology. Case had acquired the patent rights to use two other ingenious inventions, combining them into his own machine.

His advertising says that he is a "practical Thresher" who has been engaged in manufacturing and using threshing machines for the last seventeen years. Quickly doing the subtraction, it seems that Case says he has been in business since 1831.

The Early Years

The first threshers were made of wood with iron fittings. By the mid 1850's, the first significant mechanical improvements appeared. The Bessemer process for making steel was introduced to America about 1855 and allowed some of the moving parts to be manufactured from steel. Important improvements in reapers and mowers also had an impact on the development of threshers. By the 1860's a mower had been developed that would cut, bundle and tie the crop in a neat sheaf. These bundles could easily be fed into the improved thresher.

The earlier threshers were powered by hand or by a waterwheel if one was available. The next improvement was to power the thresher by horses or mules, walking a treadmill. This sort of operation was limited to one or two horses, the maximum number that would fit on the treadmill at a time. And with just one or two horses, the size of the thresher was limited by the horsepower provided.

The "ground hog" thresher was the first practical device to mechanize the process of cleaning grain, able to separate up to about 200 bushels of wheat in a day. *J. I Case*

Here's a pretty typical threshing scene from the mid 1930s, with two bundle wagons serving a medium-sized thresher powered by a sturdy tractor. *John Deere*

Right, this ad, in numerous variations, appeared as a handbill and an advertisement in the farm papers of the Midwest about 1850. *J. I Case*

RACINE

1848   **1848**

Threshing Machine Works.

J. I. CASE, - - - PROPRIETOR.

Having purchased of H. A. Pitts the right to manufacture and use his Patent revolving apron, in my *improved* Wemple Machine, and to manufacture Pitts' Patent Separator, and having added several important improvements to my Separator and Horse Power during the past season, I am prepared to supply all who wish to purchase a Lever or Tread Power Threshing Machine, with a very superior article of either kind. Being a practical Thresher and having been engaged in manufacturing and using Threshing Machines for the last seventeen years, and devoted my particular attention to improving and perfecting one just suited to the wants of the Western Farmer; I am now prepared to warrant my Machines the best in use. I except none, be they manufactured east or west.

TERMS OF PAYMENT.

TREAD MACHINE.

Fifty dollars on delivery of machine (freight or ware-house charges if any;) seventy five dollars on the first day of November; one hundred dollars on the first day of January; and sixty-five dollars on the first day of October following—all with interest.

LEVER MACHINE.

Fifty dollars on delivery of machine (freight and ware-house charges if any;) seventy-five dollars on the first day of November; ninety dollars on the first day of January; and the balance on the first day of October following—all with interest.

A deduction of ten per cent. on all sums over fifty dollars paid down for either machine.

From the Wisconsin Farmer.

We have in a former number of the Farmer, noticed Mr. Case's Threshing Machine Establishment. We believe this is the largest establishment of the kind in the west. To those who are acquainted with the work of these machines, it is unnecessary to say anything in their praise. We believe these machines take the precedence of all others whenever they can be procured. We are told by those who have used them that they are the most profitable machines that can be used, both for the employer and the employed—that one machine has earned over $1200 during the season of threshing.

Mr. C. also keeps on hand and for sale, the most improved kinds of Lever Power. His Separators are the best in use. Mr. C. has been a practical thresher some fifteen years, and knows how to get up threshing machines just right. We would advise all interested to give him a call, examine his machines, and judge for themselves. We have no doubt that whoever does so, will agree with us in the opinion we have expressed.

The great and increasing demand for my Threshing Machines, has induced me to enlarge my Establishment, attach an Iron Furnace, and put in Steam Power. For the last three years I have not been able to supply more than one-half the orders I have received for Machines; but I have now the largest and most commodious shops west of Buffalo, and hope in future to be able to supply all who may wish a superior Threshing Machine. My lumber is all of the best quality, seasoned perfectly, and put together in a workmanlike manner by the best of mechanics. I have formerly purchased my castings from other shops, where they make all kinds of castings commonly made in doing a general foundry business; consequently I have sometimes had good castings, and sometimes poor. Having my own Furnace, I shall now make my own castings, and see that none but the very best brands of machinery iron are used in them, thereby insuring the purchaser against expense and loss from breakage of bad castings. I am manufacturing and have for sale my

IMPROVED WEMPLE MACHINE, WITH CLIMAX HORSE POWER,

PITT'S PATENT SEPARATOR,

As manufactured by J. A. Pitts, of Buffalo, (also as formerly made by Marvin Hughes, of Kenosha,) with important improvements on both Machines. Some of the above Machines will be geared and others run with jack and belt, so as to suit the fancies of all purchasers. My price for either of the above Machines, at the shop, is $115 with drum cylinder, and $335 with Iron cylinder. I will also have for sale my

IMPROVED TWO-HORSE TREAD POWER MACHINE,

with Separator; price $200 without wagon for the horse-power, and $335 with wagon. My two-horse Tread Machine, if well attended in good grain, will thresh and clean nicely from 200 to 350 bushels of Wheat in a day, or twice that quantity of Oats. The Lever Power Machine I will warrant capable of threshing and cleaning, in the best manner, all that can be got to it. Should you wish either of the above described Machines, I will suggest the necessity of your forwarding your order early so as to secure one in season. If you know of any one in your vicinity who wishes to purchase a Threshing Machine, you will confer a favor on him, his neighbors and myself, by inducing him to examine my Machines before purchasing elsewhere.

CASTINGS FURNISHED FOR ALL KINDS OF MACHINERY, AND REPAIRING DONE ON SHORT NOTICE.

A. C. Sandford, Printer,   Advocate Office, Racine.

Please Post Conspicuously, or hand to some one interested in having a good Machine in your neighborhood.

The power sweep, a circular wheel that could be powered by as many as a dozen horses at a time, offered the first big jump in horsepower. Offsetting the power wheel with a power sweep arrangement such as the Woodbury Power Wheel or the Dingee Sweep offered some flexibility as well as a significant increase in power. This allowed threshing manufacturers to design equipment with a much larger capacity. According to the biography of the Case corporation *Full Steam Ahead*, the Eclipse thresher introduced by Case in 1869 could turn out 1,000 bushels of grain in a ten hour day. The next quantum

Barrett & Company's Patent Iron Thrashing Machine, 1853.

Below, **straw stacker attachment, 1899.**

Barrett and Co.'s Patent Iron Thrashing Machine.

Early thresher with "horsepower" drive, 1853.

leap in thresher development would be the advent of steam power on the farm.

Steaming Ahead

As the threshing machines grew larger and larger, with more of the manufacturing production focused on steam powered machines, the Case company decided to abandon manufacture of its smaller horse-powered threshing units. It seemed reasonable and practical to turn the manufacture of its older, smaller threshers to another company, and the Belle City Manufacturing Company was formed to handle this segment of the market.

Set up in 1862 and wholly controlled by employees of the J. I. Case Threshing Machine Company, Belle City built threshers powered by two or four horses. Eventually the Belle City thresher was found to be the optimal thresher for power units

built by the International Harvester Corporation. Years later the IHC took the entire production output of Belle City threshers.

About the same time that threshers were moving from horse power to steam power, another significant improvement in thresher design was taking place. The Eclipse thresher, first introduced in 1869, moved the grain along on a canvas belt. Paired with a small stationary steam engine, it did a creditable job in harvesting a crop. But in 1880 a new and greatly improved thresher was introduced, one that featured crank-driven, internal racks that tossed and shook the grain as it moved along. Named The Agitator, it quickly became known as the best machine on the market.

While the J. I. Case Threshing Machine Company was an industry leader, it did not have the thresher market all to themselves. The Belle City

Early hand-cranked thresher, with simple "groundhog"
cylinder and fanning mill, 1853.

Early bagging attachment, 1899.

Cylinder and concaves, 1899.

Company was making smaller threshers for the Midwestern market. Other important threshing machine builders in the 1880's included Nichols & Shepard, Aultman-Taylor and Company and Buffalo Pitts. But all of these companies would eventually be absorbed by other manufacturers.

Milestones in Thresher Development
- 1788 Scottish millwright Andrew Meikle received a Letters Patent for a threshing machine. Meikle machines are the earliest threshers imported to America.
- 1791 First American patent was granted for a threshing machine, issued to Samuel Mulliken of Philadelphia. (*The Grain Harvesters*, Quick and Buchele)
- 1830 The Pitt brothers, Hiram and John, developed and patented the belt or track type thresher to improve their own threshing business.
- 1831 Threshers were introduced into Ohio. (Ibid.)
- 1842 Jerome Increase Case headed west with six Groundhog threshers.
- 1844 J. I. Case built and successfully tested a thresher which combined a flail and a fanning mill. He built a factory in Racine, Wisconsin to build threshers.
- 1845 Jacob Wemple patented a thresher which combined a bull thresher with a fanning mill. He sold his patent to Hiram Pitts, who in turn sold his rights to J. I. Case.
- 1855 Introduction of the Bessemer process in America. Thresher parts could now be manufactured of steel, a big improvement over cast-iron.
- 1856 A steel drum and iron cylinders were added to the Case thresher.
- 1858 John Nichols of Battle Creek, Michigan built a thresher which he sold under the name of "Vibrator."

Threshing rig, 1899.

Spiral beater, 1899.

Clayton & Shuttleworth's thrashing machine, 1853.

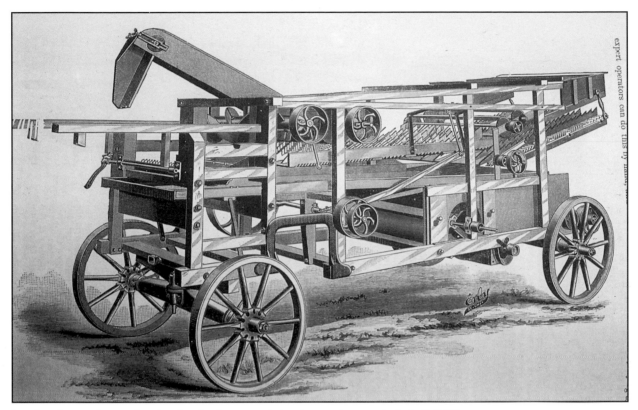

Interior view, early wooden thresher (grain pan and cleaning sections not included) 1899.

- 1862 J. I. Case Company formed the Belle City Manufacturing Company to concentrate on building small, horse-powered threshers.
- 1863 With three partners, Case formed the J. I. Case Company. The company continued to build and improve threshers.
- 1867 The Aultman & Taylor Company of Mansfield, Ohio introduced a superior thresher also marketed as the "Vibrator." (In 1920 the Aultman & Taylor Company would become part of Allis Chalmers.)
- 1869 J. I. Case began work on a steam traction machine and the first machine "Old Number 1" made its debut. (Old Number 1 is now in the collection at the Smithsonian.) Steam traction was first used to pull multiple plows, but it quickly came in to widespread use to power a thresher.

- 1869 The introduction of the Eclipse thresher, a machine which could produce 1,000 bushels of grain a day.
- 1873 An American patent was awarded to J. H. Adamson of South Australia for a combined harvester and threshing machine.
- 1876 The famous Eclipse thresher built by Case was shown at the Philadelphia Centennial Exhibition.
- 1880 The introduction of the new Agitator thresher by the Case company. The older Eclipse model was now phased out.
- 1884 Introduction of the wind-stacker for straw, invented by James Buchanan of Indianapolis, Indiana. This was an important improvement for threshermen.

Far away from Indiana, in the Down Under town of Drummartin, Victoria, a farm boy named Hugh Victor McKay built a combined stripper-harvester

Holmes Thrashing Machine, 1853.

that would cut, thresh and clean standing heads of grain. He sold his first production machine the following year, in 1885.

- 1880's Steam power was harnessed to the thresher.
- 1895 The "Sunshine" harvester, a combined harvester-thresher was manufactured in Australia. This machine would inspire Massey-Harris to build a similar machine and sell it in the American marketplace.
- 1902 The "Red River Special" was introduced, built by the Nichols & Shepard Company of Battle Creek Michigan. Replacing the *Vibrator*, it was a very popular machine. (Nichols & Shepard would merge with Oliver in 1929.)
- 1904 Case debuted their "all-steel" thresher. Lighter and more durable than wood, it was an instant success.

- 1909 H. V. McKay built the first self-propelled harvester. The Holt Company of California would introduce their own version of a self-propelled reaper-thresher the same year.
  The first commercially successful self-propelled combine was built by Holt according to historians Quick, Buchele and Quick.
- 1922 The "combined" harvester-thresher industry was well along by the time the first Case combine was finally manufactured.
- 1923 The 10,000th thresher came off the J. I. Case Threshing Company line.
- 1932 Case brought out eight combines in three sizes.It also introduced a one-man combine.
- 1953 The last Case threshing machine was built. Combines have taken over.

Barrett & Company's 4-horsepower steam engine and threshing machine, 1853.

HOW A THRESHING MACHINE WORKS

A grain threshing machine is a wonderful thing, a kind of magic that helped transform the American farm. It looks like a big metal box on wheels, and so it is. Inside this box two basic things happen, the release of the grain from the straw, and then the cleaning of the grain by separating it from the straw. It is more complicated in practice, of course, much more complicated. Here's what happens to the grain as it travels through the threshing machine, start to finish:

The bundles are tossed onto a feeder that delivers them to a set of knives, the first operation on the grain. These knives cut the twine holding the bundles together, and the bundle starts to fall apart. Within a second or so the stalks are pulled into a whirling assembly with two components, the cylinder and the concaves. The cylinder spins, usually about 1000rpm, while the concave teeth are stationary. Matching sets of steel teeth, carefully adjusted to provide clearance for individual kernels of the grain, quickly knock all the kernels out of the heads. This grain, though, is still mixed in with all the straw, but not for long.

All that straw continues a journey through the machine, being shaken, blasted by fans and

Right side of Donald Swensen's beautifully restored 1948 Red River Special, ready for action at Rollag, Minnesota. The diagonal box running along side the machine is the tailings elevator.

A view deep into the area where the cylinder teeth and the concave teeth mesh.

Right, a pile of bundles awaits the attentions of this big Yellow Boy thresher at Rollag, Minnesota.

agitated severely for about ten seconds. Several stages of screening filter out the kernels from the larger straw. Fans blast air over the grain, blowing away the lighter chaff and bits of straw remaining. Finally the kernels flow into a bin, or a wagon, or a sack and the straw falls on the ground at the end of the machine or is blown out onto a stack.

Stationary machines using this basic concept served the American farmer for a hundred years, and some still do today in the Amish communities. And while the basic idea is pretty simple, the effect on the farmer was not. This machine, as much as anything, made it possible for farmers to prosper. It takes a good sized crew to serve one, but that crew can clean a thousand bushels of grain in a single day. That allowed farmers to start growing thousands, instead of dozens, of bushels. And when that happened, the days of the tiny subsistence farm were numbered.

Steam vs Gas Threshing

Steam power was a wonderful thing and brought large scale production, efficiency, economy, and prosperity to many American farmers. Many old-timers remember that time with fondness, and you can still see these big engines at work at farm shows around the nation.

There were problems with steam powered machines, though. The engines were very heavy, weighing several tons and often they broke through

50

The feeder section from this old wooden Yellow Boy thresher has been rebuilt. The fence down the middle is common to large threshers, an accessory to help keep the flow of bundles into the cylinder orderly and properly oriented.

bridges. Sparks from the stack sometimes set fire to the standing grain. Occasionally a boiler overheated and blew up, killing the operator and any nearby help. But the factor that finally finished the steam rigs was the cost, about $110 per day for a full custom threshing crew back in 1908. And that didn't include the cost of repairs, interest, taxes, or depreciation—just the direct costs of operation. All of it had to be paid back at the rate of about three cents per bushel. That made custom threshermen well-organized, highly efficient, cost-conscious men.

Basic Layout

Let's assume you've got a grain crop to harvest, a nice big thresher in the barn, and a sturdy old Farmall F-30 tractor to provide the power. Let's also assume you also have some willing neighbors and family—and not a clue about what happens inside that mysterious big box called a threshing machine. If you're going to run it, you better know how it all works, so here's the short course:

Feeder Components

The threshing process begins with the feeder, a set of belts or canvases that carry the bundles of grain into the machine. These belts move at a speed designed to keep the cylinder (the most important part of the machine) from getting clogged or jammed with too much straw—"slugging" the machine is the traditional expression.

The bundle-pitchers should keep the feeder filled, with one bundle following another, head-first, and without gaps between the bundles. But the bundles need to be spread out evenly for the threshing

Feeder section for a McCormick-Deering thresher.

process to work properly, so as the grain bundles enter the machine several components prepare them for processing.

Carrier Rake

The carrier rake is a kind of conveyor belt that carries the bundles into the machine. On some models this is just a canvas belt, normally with wooden slats attached for extra traction. On others it is like a ladder on chains or a metal link belt. In both, the drive wheels are linked to the drivetrain for the whole machine, controlling the speed with which fresh bundles are fed into the thresher.

Band Cutter

The harvesting process normally (but not always) delivers the grain in bundles tied with twine to the threshing machine—hardly the best way to supply the cylinder and its wide rows of interlocking teeth. So each bundle begins its journey through the threshing machine at the band cutter. These are really wicked-looking knives with large, jagged teeth, driven by an adjustable Pitman arm and link assembly. While the machine is running, these knives flash up and down rapidly, cutting the twine on each bundle of grain and releasing the straw. Be careful around these knives—more than one drunken "bundle-pitcher" has fallen into the feeder and "slugged" the machine the hard way!

These whirring knives are self sharpening on some machines, like the later Case models, and begin the spreading process that continues for the next three feet or so of travel into the machine.

Straw Shoe

Above the bundle cutter is a set of long metal fingers that spread the loose straw out, getting it ready to enter the cylinder where the actual threshing will occur. The round bundle (about 16 inches in diameter as it is tossed on the feeder) quickly becomes a flat, loose mass of straw about 2 inches thick and about 24 inches wide (depending on the size of the cylinder on the machine).

As thresher design evolved over 100 years, some quite ingenious developments were added, and one was a trip mechanism on the straw shoe. If you or one of your clumsy assistants overload the feeder, the heavy supply of straw will push up on the straw shoe, causing the mechanism to trip and disconnect the feed rakes. That gives the cylinder a chance to catch up with the load and gives you a chance to either correct your error or insult the offending bundle pitcher.

Upper Feed Rake and Feed Pan

The crop is gradually and progressively forced through the machine, a process that takes around 10 to 15 seconds. Once the bundles are cut, a set of serrated bars push the material along. This assembly is called the upper feed rake. It is another oscillating component, linked to the same part of the drivetrain that operates the band cutter. When too much material enters the feeder and the straw rake sensor trips, the upper feed rake disconnects, too.

Flashing knives cut the twine on each bundle as it enters the thresher at the end of the feeder section. These knives not only release the bundles but start to spread the straw out into an even layer before entering the cylinder. Keep your hands out of this part of the machine.

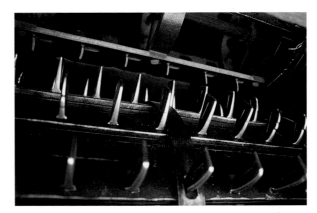

From the separator boss's perch up on top of the machine, you can look down into the feeder where the bundles enter the cylinder. The camera's flash freezes the action as the chaff starts to fly and the grain is sucked into the threshing teeth of the cylinder and concaves.

These teeth are forged steel and artfully designed. They are also polished from years of use and the impacts of millions of kernels of grain.

Below the feed rake is another set of teeth, pushing on the crop—the feed pan. It also pushes the crop deeper into the machine. The very end of the feed pan sometimes includes a set of thin metal guides called retarder fingers that function like a comb, completing the process of aligning and spreading the straw just before the crop is fed to the whirling cylinder.

With the feed rake above and the feed pan below, the crop is sucked into a mechanical transport system that dislodges the kernels of grain from the heads and separates them from the straw.

Pitman

Much of the work of the thresher is done with a kind of ratcheting motion by components that rock back and forth. The conversion of rotary motion delivered by the belt to the main pulley is accomplished by Pitman arms—simple linkages that connect a wheel of some sort (a gear, a crank disk, a fly wheel, or similar rotating part) to another component that is free to travel in a reciprocal linear way. The connecting rod in an automobile engine is an example of this kind of part, converting the linear motion of the piston on one end of the rod to the rotary motion of the crankshaft.

Governor

Some late threshers include a governor control; if the speed of the machine drops too low for proper threshing, this governor will disengage the carrier rake and halt the feeding of bundles.

Feeder Adjustment

The feeder assembly and all its components deliver the grain to the cylinder.

Some feeders are adjustable to feed the crop high or low on the cylinder, providing more or less threshing action—depending on the kind of grain and the condition of the crop. A dry crop threshes best with the feeder set to deliver to the lower part of the cylinder. When the grain is tangled and wet, a feeder that can be adjusted to feed to the upper portion of the cylinder will allow the crop to be combed, setting it up for cleaner action as it goes through the teeth of the cylinder and concaves. Rice, alfalfa, and clover are particularly hard to thresh and such a feeder adjustment was a big improvement for farmers of these crops when it was introduced.

On primitive, early threshers, the feeder is a pretty simple device that requires a lot of skill from the bundle-pitchers to keep from slugging the machine; later models provide mechanical safeguards to maintain an even, efficient flow of crop into the thresher.

Cylinder And Threshing Components

Actual threshing of the grain occurs in just a fraction of a second, as the straw is sucked into the interlocking teeth of the cylinder and matching concaves.

One of the problems with restoring old threshers is that the common use of wood tends to decay overtime, like this old wooden component.

Hanger brackets support the grain pan and cleaning shoe, both of which oscillate back and forth inside the machine.

Virtually every threshing machine uses friction belts to transmit power to its components.

A twist in the belt will reverse the direction of rotation—essential for some components.

Threshing Cylinder and Teeth

The cylinder is nothing more than a precision steel version of the old wood "ground hog"—the chunk of tree truck with pegs hammered into holes. In the more modern version found in the thresher (and in most combines, too) the log has been replaced by a heavy fabricated steel drum that is typically from 28 inches to 60 inches wide and 20 inches to 36 inches in diameter. The cylinder design is normally an open affair, with lateral bars about 3/8 inch thick supporting rows of sturdy forged steel teeth, and with end caps of forged steel or cast-iron. The cylinder rotates around a heavy steel shaft driven by the main pulley.

The teeth are really massive forged steel pins about 4 inches long overall, about 2 inches of which projects above the thick steel bar. A tremendous amount of study and experimentation went into the design of these teeth, with manufacturers making claims and counterclaims about the virtues of one design or another.

Typical speed for the cylinder is about 1000rpm, plus or minus 50rpm; this is the design speed for the whole machine, and part of the skill of operating a thresher is the ability to adjust the speed of the tractor pulley to attain this figure.

At 1000 rpm the top speed of the cylinder teeth will be about 60 miles per hour or about 5,300 feet per minute—and the speed of travel for those cylinder teeth have a lot to do with how well the crop is threshed.

The threshing is accomplished by a kind of combined combing and rubbing action as the heads of grain are "sucked" into the machine by the rotation of the cylinder. The teeth engage the crop, pulling it

Each manufacturer had its own ideas about the most effective design for the chaffer section.

down and around the cylinder, and forcing it between gaps in the stationary concave teeth.

Concaves and Stationary Teeth

The so-called concaves are a set of stationary teeth exactly like those on the cylinder, forged steel pins with threaded ends that are retained by nuts and lock-washers on stationary steel bars. These rows of stationary teeth are attached to steel bars of massive construction, and individual rows of teeth can be added or removed, depending on the kind of crop and its condition; threshing peas or peanuts requires a very different set up than that needed for barley or oats!

Teeth

The gap between the cylinder teeth and the concave teeth is adjustable; the concave assembly can be raised or lowered relative to the cylinder. That's important because the gap should be just a bit larger than the typical kernel of the crop—and that size varies from one kind of grain to another, and from one kind of growing conditions to another. You can have scrawny little kernels of barley one year, big fat kernels the next. Too large a gap will let grain stay in the heads, unthreshed and wasted, and too tight a gap will clog the cylinder and break the kernels.

The action of a properly adjusted cylinder and concaves on the grain will thresh about 95 percent of the kernels from the heads. The grain pours out of the cylinder area like a little hail storm, most falling through the concaves and the finger grates just "down stream" from the cylinder.

Finger Grates

A set of about 40 long, slender steel springs guide the straw off the cylinder as it flies from the back of the spinning cylinder. These are called finger grates. These spring steel rods guide the straw up to the beater while allowing any grain kicked off the cylinder to fall through toward the grain pan below.

Grain Pan

The threshed grain gushes off the cylinder in a torrent, through the bars of the stationary concaves—most falling on a smooth steel sheet at the bottom of the machine, the grain pan. This large sheet metal component is tilted toward the back of the machine, allowing the crop to flow downward. This pan is mechanically agitated in a rolling, back and forth motion that moves the grain back toward screens to be collected. This is the easy part of the threshing process.

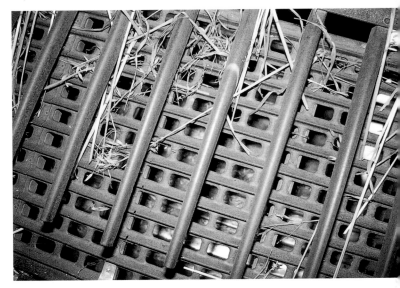

The cleaning section of a thresher is essentially a set of three "filters," or screens, with the coarsest (seen here) on top.

Here is the chaffer section of a thresher, an intermediate screen. The design of the apertures in the sheet metal allow kernels of threshed grain to fall down for collection, while the larger, lighter straw is carried along toward the rear.

Beater

Some of the grain will stick in the heads, perhaps 5 or 10 percent—and since this can be the farmer's profit margin on the crop, it is essential to get it all. The *beater* is the first of several stages of processing that goes after this remaining bit of crop.

The beater is another rotary component, spinning in the opposite direction from the cylinder. This component typically has four large "wings" or baffles that clean the material remaining on the cylinder teeth and help redirect the flow of straw and residual grain back through the threshing machine. It catches the grain that flies upward off the back of the cylinder and knocks it down toward the straw racks and grain pan below. As the straw comes off the beater onto the straw racks, the actual threshing process is finished and virtually all the grain is loosened from the straw; now the separating process begins.

The blower at the rear of the thresher provides a flow of air to remove the light chaff, dust, and bits of straw from the grain. The volume of airflow is critical—adjusted by the sheet metal panels (called "blinds" on most threshers) since the rotational speed of the fan is pretty much fixed to that of the cylinder.

Separating Components

Now comes the beginning of the hard part—the third phase, separation. This part of the machine mimics the winnowing action of the old time hand threshers who used simple screens and the wind to clean the light chaff and straw from the small, dense grain kernels.

Straw Racks

The first part of the separation process begins as the straw, with a fair amount of grain still mixed in, comes off the back of the spinning cylinder and is tossed onto the straw racks or straw walkers. This portion of the threshing machine agitates the straw while moving it back through the machine. The agitation is provided by rows of serrated, angled bars (in most but not all machines) that push and prod each piece of straw, kicking loose any residual kernels. The action is a frenzy of ratcheting teeth, lifting and pushing and prodding each length of straw along the line, with plenty of room for the grain to escape. Virtually every kernel (normally over 98 percent, often very close to 100 percent) will be separated.

Each kernel knocked loose from the straw falls down to the long grain pan—the same part that caught all the grain coming from the spinning cylinder. The smooth sheet metal pan is tilted back toward the end of the thresher, and it, too, is agitated; this moves the grain in a steady stream toward the bin and the bag.

The grain pan and the straw racks are typically about the same size and weight, and both shimmy

Not all the grain will get threshed on the first pass through the machine, and the heads that don't end up here, at the tailings auger, to be sent up the tailings elevator (on the right) back to the cylinder for another try.

and shake like Jell-O in an earthquake. That vibration could damage the machine, so some manufacturers used the same drive components to power both parts, but in opposite directions. The result was the vibration ceased and the thresher didn't keep trying to hop all over the lot.

Cleaning Components

As the threshed grain slides and bounces back down the long, smooth grain pan, large quantities of chaff, tiny bits of straw, and weed seeds come along for the ride. Since the farmer gets "docked" for this residue, it pays to get rid of it all. That's what the cleaning section components do.

Conveyor Sieve

As the grain and chaff mixture slides down the pan, they encounter the first cleaning action after about 15 feet of travel (in a full sized machine), the conveyor sieve. This is a grate attached to the end of the grain pan; the bars of the grate are adjustable. That lets the operator set the machine up to suit the condition of the crop—which varies from one field to another, and from one day to another—to minimize the amount of grain getting blown out with the chaff. Air blasts up and back through this first grate, blowing away most of the chaff while permitting the heavy kernels of grain to drop down to the next phase of the operation, the second cleaning on the adjustable shoe sieve.

The gap between the grates are quite large on the conveyor sieve (also know as the "chaffer"), allowing the grain to drop a few inches onto another cleaning component, the screen. All the chaff would fall along with the grain except for the high volume of air blowing up through the sieve, carrying away the chaff.

Grain flows straight up from the bottom of the machine to the top of this elevator assembly, and into the hopper of the weigher. When the weight of the grain trips the catch and counterweight, the hopper drains into a duct and flows down to the bagger or to a wagon parked alongside the thresher.

While the separator boss wasn't looking, we popped open the door at the back of the machine and grabbed this shot. The flash has frozen the straw flowing out the back of the straw racks, into the intake for the wind-stacker. Below the straw you can see the chaff and small fragments of straw being lifted off the grain, nearly all of which is falling down onto the adjustable sieve, or "shoe" below. Now, quick, let's button the panel up again before we get in trouble.

Extension Chaffer

Inevitably, some heads of grain will sneak through the cylinder unthreshed—and once onto the straw racks, they all think they have escaped. In some basic threshing machines they will go all the way through, the grain ending up in the straw pile. Just before they make a break for freedom, though, they are intercepted in the more modern machines by an extension chaffer or grate designed to intercept these wayward kernels and send them back to the cylinder.

The angle of the baffles can be adjusted to keep the volume of lost grain to a minimum. These unthreshed heads of grain drop through the extension chaffer, down to the tailings auger, and are carried back to the cylinder for another trip through the machine.

Cleaning Shoe

The second and final cleaning phase is accomplished by two screens that essentially filter the grain from any residual straw. These screens are each made

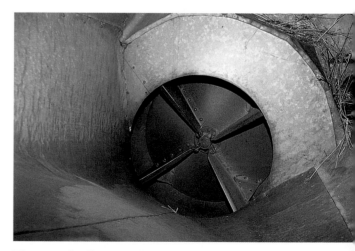

The straw finally arrives here, at the far end of the thresher. That's not a fan but a kind of pump for the straw that collects the material and blasts it out the long tube called the "wind stacker" and onto the straw pile.

62

Weigher/bagger attachments were offered as factory options and aftermarket accessories. The weigher uses a counterweight system (set here to 23 pounds) to measure the flow of grain through the machine. As the hopper fills, then trips at the predetermined weight, a counter records the amount.

from two sheets of perforated steel; by adjusting the sheets relative to each other, the openings can be made larger or smaller to suit the crop. This "cleaning shoe," as it is called, is tilted, agitated, and is cleaned by the blast of air from the fan, all helping separate the clean grain from the straw, chaff, and dirt.

Under Blast Fan

The fan, or "under-blast" fan simulates the age-old use of the wind to blow away the light chaff from the heavy grain. The design of the fan is typically quite simple, no more that half a dozen simple paddles arranged on a shaft driven (along with every-thing else) by the drivetrain powered by the tractor. The amount of airflow is easily adjustable by the use of simple sheet metal doors or blinds. These pivot, allowing greater or lesser amounts of air to enter the fan inlet housing.

This airflow may not be highly pressurized, but large volumes are moved, directed upward through (normally) sheet metal ducting to the cleaning screens and sieves. The idea is to get enough airflow to blow away the light chaff, dust, dirt, and residual straw, but not so much that the grain gets blasted out at the same time. Adjusting these blinds is part of the setup procedure and the art of the separator boss.

Grain gushes from Bill Vavak's big Advance-Rumley into a wagon.

Tailings Auger

A percentage of the grain will inevitably fail to thresh properly—and will normally be intercepted by the extension chaffer. When these clusters of grain, too big to get through the screens in the cleaning shoe, fall through, bounce off the tailboard, and land in the tailings auger, they are about to get a free ride back to the head of the line. The tailings auger collects this material, moves it to an elevator, and sends it back for threshing again.

Weed Screen

Now, we don't grow weeds here on our place, but some farmers do—I am not sure why—and the seeds get threshed along with the grain. The big seeds get caught by the first screens in the cleaning shoe, but the small ones try to sneak into the sack or bin along with the wheat, oats, or barley by falling

through the larger openings on the cleaning shoe. Thresher manufacturers generally provide a weed screen with mesh smaller than the grain being threshed to eliminate these tiny seeds, and they fall out the bottom of the thresher onto the ground.

Grain Auger

At last, the clean grain rolls down the inclined face of the weed screen in a cascade, accumulating at the very bottom of the threshing machine in the grain auger. Here it is quickly carried up and away, out of the thresher, by an auger system.

Weigher

Getting an accurate measurement of the weight of the crop is important to everybody involved in the threshing. The farmer, of course, needs to know what he has to sell, but the threshing ring or the custom

Bagging attachment for a Case thresher. A simple gate valve diverts the flow of grain from one bag to the other. As soon as one fills, the lever is switched, the full bag removed and sewn, and a fresh bag attached by clips to the spout.

Detail, wind-stacker; when that pulley is powered with a belt, the wind-stacker can be set up to oscillate back and forth, automatically building the straw pile.

thresher, too, in many cases need to know because they will "settle up" on the basis of the size of the crop. As the grain is carried up and out by the grain auger and elevator components, it passes through a device that weighs the grain in small batches, then records the weight automatically. These weighers were sometimes offered as factory options on some machines after the turn of the century, but normally were purchased as "aftermarket extras."

Loader

Now the clean and weighed grain is ready for the bag or the bin. In nearly all machines, it is next carried vertically by an elevating mechanism and allowed to flow back down through a spout, either into the back of a grain wagon as loose bulk grain, or into a bagging attachment.

Bagging Attachment

Bagged grain was the standard method in use in the West, right up to recent years, while bulk grain handling has been standard in the Midwest. While you could try bagging grain direct from the spout, it would be messy. A simple bagging attachment holds two jute bags, one being filled, the other empty. As the first fills, a lever flips a diverter plate, sending the

Some wind stackers, like this one on a Case 26-inch machine, could be set up to swing back and forth, automatically. That made for a big, even straw pile and even less work for the crew.

flow of grain to the empty bag. Some bagging attachments include a "tallying" device to count the number of bags filled automatically.

Wind Stacker

Early threshing machines delivered the straw to the back of the machine and dumped it all on the ground where a crew of boys and men with pitch forks scurried around trying to keep it all under control. The "wind stacker," a blower and duct assembly, made this tough, dirty job easy enough for a small boy.

The wind stacker adds a large fan to the very end of the machine, and an adjustable ductwork (often called the "straw chute") that can be easily cranked into position to place the straw just about anywhere within about a 20 foot radius. Some of these windstackers even motorized the straw chute so it slowly oscillated back and forth, building a large, even, tidy straw pile behind the machine. Some of these piles could reach immense size, up to about 20 feet tall and 50 feet long, around the back of the machine.

"Thrashing" Day

There were about 25 to 30 men on the threshing crew, including waterboys. Promptly at 11:30 the separator boss called a halt for dinner, and believe me, the men were hungry by that time!

The noontime threshing meal was normally the highlight of the whole day! The women of the farm started work early in the morning. All of them kept flocks of chickens and many would be sacrificed for these dinners! I can still remember the iced tea and fried chicken we got at those meals, and where I grew up we almost always got fried chicken as part of that noon meal.

There was an abundance of food, normally served on a screened porch where tables would be set for all the crew. Generally one woman or two would stand by with a something to keep the flies away from the food—flies were pretty bad at that time of year. But the food was good and clean, and the women made every effort to keep it clean.

The normal day started bright and early— Dad rolled out about 4 a.m. and I got up about 5—with morning chores, then we went to the farm where the day's threshing was to be done. We couldn't really get started until 9:30 or 10 a.m. many times, though, because the grain was still damp from the evening dew.

The man that owned the thresher and the tractor was the boss. Everybody counted on him to keep things going and under control, even though it wasn't his farm we were working on. If he signaled for things to stop, you stopped right then! And when he said "go" you better be ready to go!

After a year or two as waterboy, I advanced to the job of bundle-pitcher at the age of 15 or 16. That was a big achievement for me! The bundle-pitcher's job is to use a pitchfork to take the bundles of grain from the shock and toss them up into the wagon where another fellow would load them.

Some of these guys would take it easy on us but others liked to load the wagon to capacity; that meant you had to toss the bundles up higher. These men were good loaders, but they all expected each bundle to come up in the rack with the heads in and the butts out, just right, every time! You could get chewed out if you didn't do it right!

After a while you learn to do two bundles at a time, and some could do half a shock, but the teamsters didn't usually appreciate that because they wanted to load each just right. Actually, that was quite a skill—as I discovered when I advanced to driving a team on a bundle wagon! You had to drive that wagon maybe three quarters of a mile across the fields and some pretty uneven ground—and you didn't want the wagon to upset. That happened on occasion, but not often!

My father always kept big Belgian horses— we called them "the old gray mares"—and they were always the choice team for a bundle wagon. That's because they knew when to move from shock to shock with just a quiet voice command; all you had to say was "Now, Nellie!" Then they would move up, into position with the wagon right by the next shock, and you wouldn't even have to touch the reins.

Driving a bundle wagon across uneven farmland was an important skill, but so was putting the wagon into position alongside the feeder. You couldn't get too close or the thresher was likely to get bumped, and if you were too far away then you'd have a hard time hitting the feeder every time and you'd have a lot of bundles land on the ground. The older men would teach you how to do it, and then you were on your own!

You needed a real steady team of horses; with all the noise and vibration from the belts and the separator, a green horse would spook or bolt.

It was important for the men tossing bundles into the feeder to keep an even flow. Sometimes, out of sheer "orneryness," somebody would intentionally slug the machine just to get a rest. Man, that separator boss would get angry then!

John Slauter

The wind stacker made life a lot easier and a lot more pleasant for the boys working the straw pile. Previously, the straw got dumped on the ground and had to be piled by hand, with a pitchfork; once the wind-stacker came into vogue, managing the straw pile became, literally, a child's job.

The wind-stacker can be adjusted to direct the straw just about anywhere within a very wide radius, and can build a pile over 20 feet high.

Wind-stacker controls.

FEED ~ THRESH ~ SEPARATE ~ CLEAN

Better and Faster With a CASE

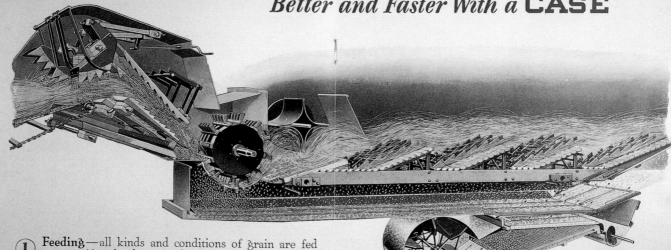

① **Feeding**—all kinds and conditions of grain are fed more uniformly than can be done by human hands.

② **Threshing** — kernels are swiftly and thoroughly loosened from the heads by the all-steel cylinder and concaves.

③ **Separating** — most of the grain separates immediately through the concaves and finger grates, and the last few kernels are shaken out by the vigorous agitation of the straw rack.

④ **Cleaning** — dust, chaff and weed seeds are thoroughly cleaned from sound grain by the underblast fan and sieves of special Case design.

Cutaway view of threshing process. *J. I. Case*

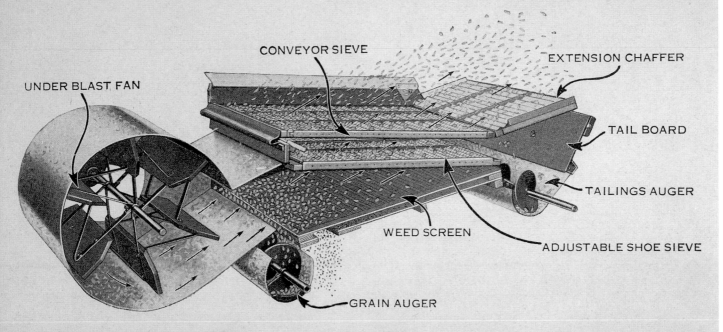

CONVEYOR SIEVE

EXTENSION CHAFFER

UNDER BLAST FAN

TAIL BOARD

TAILINGS AUGER

WEED SCREEN

ADJUSTABLE SHOE SIEVE

GRAIN AUGER

Thorough Cleaning
The Fourth Operation of Good Threshing

Cutaway view of cleaning section of threshing machine. *J. I. Case*

HOW TO RUN A THRESHING MACHINE

The first consideration is the question of where to set up to do the work. If the straw is going to be used for stock bedding or feed, you will probably want it close to the barn, or maybe inside; that is typical in the East and Midwest. Out in Nebraska and the Great Plains, the straw pile will probably get burned—and you don't want that happening anywhere near the barns, so the threshing will be done out in the field, close to the crop.

Typically, you look for a wide, level spot. It needs to be wide so the teams can maneuver the bundle wagons in and out of position, and the grain wagon will need room, too.

The ground itself doesn't have to be perfectly level, but the thresher must—so you either find a level spot, or dig holes for the wheels. You will probably dig holes for the wheels anyway, but the less shovel work required, the better.

Threshing is dirty work on the best of days, so you try to have the straw and chaff blow away from the machine and crew, as

This big Advance-Rumley thresher belongs to Bill Vavak, an old-time Nebraska thresherman. Bill has been saving and exhibiting threshers at Camp Creek, just outside Waverly, for years.

Bill Vavak and helpers inspect the Advance-Rumley before belting up.

much as possible—so the machine is sited with the prevailing winds in mind. If the wind shifts and you have a straw pile that starts to build on top of the machine, you are likely to shut down and move the whole rig.

Belting up

First, make sure you've got a tractor that can handle your thresher. Lots of members of the Brotherhood of American Threshermen swear by the steady power of steam and will tell you a steam

What's wrong with this picture? Well, our hero is far too clean—but the day is young, and he will be filthy soon enough. The separator boss inspects and adjusts the thresher before each day's run, and at every halt.

engine is the perfect power source for threshing work. Other veterans of the threshing wars will swear by Avery, John Deere, and all the other gasoline and distillate tractors that became popular beginning about the time of World War I. The smaller threshers, with cylinders of about 22-inch size, can be powered with a Farmall F-20, while the moderate sized threshers in the 30-inch class work better with a Farmall 15-30 (15 horsepower on the drawbar, 30 horsepower at the pulley) or equivalent.

Threshing is a business that uses a lot of belts—a dozen or so on some machines, plus the big one that transmits power from the tractor flywheel. This latter belt is the most critical and causes the most problems, and you will frequently see apprentice threshermen at farm shows trying to get the belt to stay on the machine, with little success.

A long belt has some real virtues and was, and is, preferred. The long belt makes alignment easier; it's weight helps prevent slipping and sliding on the pulleys. On steam engines, it keeps sparks a little further from the straw (and fire was a real problem during threshing days). Also, a long belt gets the tractor a bit further out of the way of the teams maneuvering into the feeder, too. Long belts are good belts.

You'll often see a twist in the main belt. The primary reason for the twist is to reverse the direction of rotation, to give the machine power in the right direction. A steam engine can run just as well forward or back, but a gasoline engine has only one direction of rotation—sometimes the wrong direction for threshing machines.

The twist serves another, secondary function: it reduces the flapping of that long belt when the wind

75

Setting Up

We threshed until I was in the 6th grade, give or take, so I've seen threshing machines set up a number of times.

First Rule: Set up the machine so the feeder is pointing into the wind. That way, all chaff is blown away from the machine. Those poor guys pitching bundles into the feeder have a tough enough time without getting itchy chaff down their shirts, too. If the wind shifts, take a coffee break and re-set the machine.

All the threshermen I knew would put the machine into position, then dig half-moon shaped holes for all four wheels to roll into. When the holes were dug they'd roll the machine and let the wheels drop in. It does two things:

1) It anchors the machine against the tension of the main drive belt.

2) It lowers the machine slightly so that when getting to the end of the load on the bundle rack (hay rack, wagon, or whatever you want to call it), the men don't have to pitch the bundles up so high to the feeder.

After the tractor is lined-up and the belt runs true, you may want to drive it forward and dig holes for the tractor wheels, particularly if the brakes don't hold too well. (Sure, you can carry blocks to chock the wheels, but that's all the more stuff to drag along.)

I remember taking the tongue out of the thresher. That got it out of the way and made it easier to clean up under the feeder. I don't remember the size of the machine, but our neighbor used his 1938 A-C WC on his and it had all the power we needed with four men pitching into the thresher. An uncle of mine used an International 15-30, as I recall, and it worked quite well. This tractor was rather hard starting, so he would put kerosene into it and run it all night, rather than try to get it started the next morning. He'd run it on gasoline when on the thresher.

Take the belts off every night and lay them in the straw racks. That way, they won't get damaged if it rains. I'm sure it also allows them to "pull back" to near their original length when the tension was relaxed.

While the machine is running, check for grain carry over. To do this, open up the door on the side opposite the straw blower. Put your arm behind the straw racks and catch some of what's coming off. Pull your arm out and check for grain. If you're getting carryover, adjust the straw racks.

Another adjustment is the air intake to the blower that sits under the machine. You've got to balance it between clean grain and blowing some out to the stack.

Get there early in the morning and service the machine. When the crew stops for lunch, service the machine. Your day will be a little bit longer than the rest of the crew.

Orrin Iseminger

Adjustments are commonplace on virtually all threshers, a necessity when crop conditions change. The amount of moisture in the crop, the stage at which it was cut, and the variety of grain, will all demand adjustments to the machine.

"Wasting Grain—
Some Facts Worth Knowing"

(From Kernels for the Starved Rooster" published in 1903 by the Aultman & Taylor Machinery Company, a thresher and steam engine builder)

*I*n a bushel of oats, 32 pounds,, there are about 60,000 kernels. In one ounce of average about there are 1,100 kernels by actual count, or one million kernels in one bushel of 60 pounds. A machine that will waste 10 kernels a minute would waste a bushel of wheat in three months, counting 26 days in a month and ten hours in a day. Of course you would not catch all the waste grain in your hand as you could only hold it under a small part of the falling chaff. Suppose the machine was 52 inches wide and your hand only 2 inches, and the grain wasted equally across the entire width. it would then take three days at the same rate for enough kernels to pass to fill a bushel measure.

In order to waste five bushels in a day of ten hours' run, there would have to be 138 kernels escape every second, or 8,240 every minute. It is very deceiving when the quantity of grain comes to be measured by the kernels. Most threshermen do all in their power to save the grain for their customers and the farmer should remember that the machine which will save every kernel has never been nor ever will be invented and that the actual waste is very small compared to the quantity threshed. The "Aultman Taylor" Separator does not waste enough grain to even fatten the Starved Rooster.

comes up. Without the twist, the belt can flop around and come off, requiring a shutdown. A shutdown will make the separator boss mad—and the bundle-pitchers happy for the rest—so it is a mixed blessing. On very windy days, you can plant a pitchfork in the ground alongside the belt, the wooden handle serving as a stop for the belt, preventing too much flapping.

Getting up to Speed

Threshing machines are designed to run within a fairly narrow speed range, typically about 1,000rpm, plus or minus 50rpm. All the fans and reciprocating and rotating components function properly at design speed, and bad things start to happen as the speed picks up or drops. The engine or tractor operator should know by ear when the belt is providing approximately the correct speed, but the separator boss will signal the tractor operator or engineer to speed up or slow down, bringing the machine up to proper rpm.

It is too noisy to be heard clearly, so a few signals are standard in the threshing business:

To speed up: the thresher boss puts one hand in the air, index finger extended upward, and makes a circling motion until the tractor powers the thresher up to speed.

To slow down: the thresher boss points downward, with a circular motion, until the speed is correct.

To stop: the thresher boss quickly crosses and uncrosses his arms at waist level. There are variations on this theme—sometimes overhead, sometimes with a lot of jumping up and down, and when disaster is about to strike, accompanied with a lot of yelling and perhaps profane expressions.

The separator boss was normally the owner of the machine. From the top of the thresher, he could see and command almost all aspects of the operation, and peek inside once in a while, to see how well the rig was working.

Besides experience and observation, a lot of threshermen used a small speed gauge to accurately measure the rotation speed of the cylinder—although this was considered cheating by some of the competition.

A Case Study

The J. I. Case Company sold more steam tractors than any other company and you'll still find many of them around, chuffing away at farm shows like the huge event held at Rollag, Minnesota, every year. A typical Case tractor of the steam era was the 25-80; the numbers indicate horsepower at the draw bar (25) and at the pulley (80). That much power takes a pretty big boiler. The 25-80 is a big machine about the size and bulk of today's largest tractors, without the speed, but with lots of brute power.

A big engine like that can handle a big threshing machine. A 40-inch Case thresher would be a good choice for a match. The whole package cost almost $4,000 new, back around 1905. The only way to pay off an investment this large would be to thresh a lot of grain. So the rig owner would try to line-up as many farms to serve as possible. For George Jackson in central Missouri in the 1930s, that would normally be about 36 farms. Each would need about one day's work.

The threshing run began for George about July 4th in that part of the country and would last for six weeks. Sometimes the rig would progress along a long line across the countryside; at the end of the season it would be secured under cover at the last farm, stored for the winter, then retrace its migration the next season.

More Advice on How to Run a Threshing Machine

First of all, the grease cups and oilers must be checked to see that they are functional and filled. The feeder chain on the bundle feeder must be checked and oiled. If the thresher is to be roaded to the field, the grease cups on the trucks need to be checked and the wheels inspected to make sure the wheel nuts are tight.

Verify that the tools are in the tool box, particularly the cylinder tooth wrench, a wheel wrench, a pipe wrench, a hammer, a pair of pliers and a large screwdriver.

A long neck oil can needs to be filled and placed in the holder. If the thresher is of a newer version, and has grease Zerk fittings, the Zerk fittings must be greased until you hear the grease "pop" or three of four good pumps are taken by the fitting.

If the thresher is in place, the windstacker needs to be cranked so that the tube is ready to deliver chaff to the straw pile. A bit of oil on the crank, the cable, and the turning gear will make the effort a bit easier.

At this point, the thresher boss needs to climb up the ladder to the topside of the thresher. The grain weigher on the top of the thresher needs to be oiled and the counter checked.

If the thresher will dump the grain into a wagon, the spout needs to be checked along with the rod to hold it in place. If a bagger is to be used, a mental note must be made to set the bagger stand before threshing.

Since the thresher boss is already on top of the machine, the inspection ports should be opened and the cylinder inspected from the top, and oiled as necessary. At the same time, the wooden slats of the shakers and sieves should be inspected and repaired as necessary. Later versions were of steel and should be okay as they were far more durable. Nevertheless, they need to be checked.

Having replaced the covers on the top of the machine and climbed down, the side inspection covers need to be opened and the guts of the machine need to be attended to from the ground. If all is well, the belt needs to be unwound from the side of the thresher, inspected, and if the laces are worn or broken, repaired. A belt splicer is used to splice the ends of the belt together, unless the belt is a continuous belt. Belts of either type are acceptable if in good condition.

If the thresher is already in place for threshing, the thresher needs to be leveled. Some threshermen like to dig the wheels in a bit and use a 6 foot long level to verify that the machine is square with the world. My grandfather, Charles Kubicek, would usually eyeball the machine or use a 6 inch level on each of the wheels to "square it up."

Next, the small belts need to be checked and repaired or replaced. If they are in good condition, they need to be placed and centered on their respective flywheels. Subsequently, the main belt needs to be laid out and repaired or replaced as needed. If it is in good order, it is given a twist. Often the main belt is 60 to 100 feet long and needs to be set off a bit from the line of approach so that the steam engine or tractor can approach and align with the flywheel.

Now, the steam engineer or the tractor driver approaches the thresher and lines-up the flywheel of the engine or tractor with the main flywheel of the thresher. An assistant on the ground then lifts one side of the belt up and over the engine/tractor flywheel and centers the belt. The engine/tractor then backs up to tighten the belt. At this point, a tentative start of the separator is in order.

The steam engine/tractor engages the clutch and the flywheel begins to turn. The thresher begins to operate with the successive sets of flywheels turning, driven by belts and flywheels.

The threshing boss inspects the thresher and may use a cylinder gage to determine the revolutions per minute of the cylinder. The usual rate is about 200 to 220 revolutions per minute. Faster speeds may move grain across the cylinder too fast and provide incomplete threshing across the sieves. In addition, the higher speed may damage the rocker arms on the shakers, the fan blades on the wind stacker and put to much tension on the smaller belts.

If all is running well, the first rack of bundles pulled by horses or tractor now approaches. The rack pitchers climb up on the rack of wheat or oats bundles, the clean grain wagon is positioned, the thresher boss climbs up on top of the thresher and threshing begins.

The rack pitchers toss the bundles lengthwise into the feeder. As the feeder chain moves the bundles toward the throat of the thresher, the knives cut the twine off the bundles and feed the grain toward the cylinder, which dislodges the grain from the head and further breaks up the straw to be fed across the shakers and sieves. Clean grain drops through the sieves, which can be adjusted to capture more or less grain and to exclude more or less chaff.

If all is working well from the top of the thresher, the thresher boss checks the belts, the rocker arms, the oilers, the quality of the grain in the wagon and the amount of grain that may be escaping in the chaff as it is blown out the windstacker. Adjustments are made as necessary.

An eye is also kept on the rack pitchers, so that the number of bundles pitched do not exceed the capacity of the machine to thresh it. A slugged machine may throw the main belt, or tear a small belt, and may bend a cylinder tooth, or break a shaker arm. As much as the threshing boss watches and manages, so does the steam engineer or tractor operator.

The rest of the day is spent feeding the machines, looking, listening, checking, adjusting and work, work, working.

Terry Kubicek

Detail, Yellow Boy thresher.

The work was sometimes very hard and often dusty and dirty, particularly for the men working on the straw pile. And the pace sometimes just wore men out, especially the hired men recruited from town. These were often drifters, hoboes, teachers or college men on summer vacation, and they were usually out of shape. But they weren't dummies, and if one happened to be pitching bundles into the feeder, there was always an easy way to get a break. All you had to do was toss a couple of extra bundles in when the separator boss wasn't looking, "slugging" the cylinder and jamming the machine. Then you'd get a breather while the jam was resolved and the machine was repaired.

Tom Coles minds the horses while the crew pours bundles into the feeder.

The Ring Is Broken

The thresher was replaced by the combine for several reasons that killed off production of the machines by the early 1950s. A few folks, including Donald Swenson of Rollag, Minnesota, continued to thresh into the 1960s, and of course a few people (mostly Amish) continue to do so today.

But the little Allis-Chalmers All-Crop combine, introduced in the 1930s, demonstrated the possibility that each farmer could harvest his own crops with his own labor—and on his own schedule. A lot of money was lost by farmers waiting for the threshing crew to arrive when wind, water, or grasshoppers arrived to take a bite out of the crop.

And, as fate decreed, most American threshing machines wore out about the same time. World War II production restrictions demanded that farmers make do with equipment like tractors and threshers for the duration. By the end of the war, just about every threshing machine in the country was suffering from loose bearings and missing teeth. Most had long exceeded their manufactured design life span and needed to be scrapped and replaced. Farmers had a choice—stick with the labor-intensive thresher or the more modern combines like the John Deere 55, the All-Crop, and equivalents. They chose the combine by acclamation. Case quit building threshers when the market dried up, early in the 1950s. Dion, in Canada, was the last builder.

During the 1950s and 1960s, the surviving and last-built threshing machines gradually wore out. Most were parked in the farm "bone yard" or were pushed in a gully or sent off to the crusher and sold for scrap. Some few thousands stayed in barns or

An Alternate View
from Raymond, Kans.

Gentlemen:

I would not hesitate to give your company a few words of appreciation regarding the wonderful Case combine we purchased from you last season. Possibly the most benefit the housewife receives from one of these is that of elimination of the tramps and undesirable help one needed to put up with when cutting wheat the old way. Two years ago when we cut wheat with the header we hauled twenty-five different men out from town.

Last year with the Case combine we employed two very respectable men who started and finished the job. We did not lose a moment's time on account of the Case combine. We cut nearly five hundred acres, while our neighbors who have machines put out by two different companies cut only two hundred and fifty acres—and then we finished three or four days sooner.

Below is a general summary of what I believe we saved in each day's run with our Case combine:

3 men 9 meals at 50c each	$ 4.50 per day
3 men-wages at $4 each	$12.00 per day
1 hired girl with meals	$3.00 per day
2 bushels. wheat per acre	
50 acres, 100 bushels	$150.00 per day
6c per bushels. on 500 bushels.	
per day for threshing	$30.00 per day
4 days straw scattering on	
50 acres at $1.50 per day	$6.00 per day
total	$205.50 per day

Mrs. Geo. Eatinger

---

equipment sheds, under cover, collecting dust and mouse nests. A few of these have been cleaned up, oiled, greased, adjusted, and rolled out for the hundreds of farm shows held annually around Canada and the United States, and in England, too. While threshing machines are mostly gone, they are not forgotten. The survivors are well-loved and a small battalion or two still serve proudly, long after the men that bought and worked them during their working lives have been harvested themselves.

Farm women especially, once they realized there was an option, welcomed the combine. The competition for best cook in the neighborhood might have been an honor, but the cost of earning it was steep, and farm women didn't particularly enjoy cooking for all those dirty men and boys on "thrashing day."

Thrashing War Story

Bascomb Clark worked the straw pile, an awful job before the development of the "wind stacker" which would blow the chaff and straw out of the machine and into a neat and reasonably orderly mound.

"On one particular occasion I remember the machine crew was crowding the 'mourners' on the straw stack to the limit, not stopping to water us more than once an hour. During this hard run it occurred to me that just a tiny twist of the tine of the fork under the drive chain might bring relief. You know that the feeder who minds his business keeps a close watch on the straw stack as well as every other part of the machine. It required fast work to move the previous question, so I gave the correct sign of distress and off came the chain! We all wondered how in thunder that chain came off that

Ardenwood Historic Farm's late model Case thresher in action. Dave Cook (doing the honors on the bagging attachment) rebuilt the machine pretty much by guess and by gosh; there are few overhaul manuals available for these machines. It gets some exercise every year at one of two annual threshing events at Ardenwood—if you show up, they might let you pitch a bundle or two.

sprocket! What you don't know in this world of trials sometimes won't disturb your conscience, especially if you are a thresherman."

Threshing Rings

The invention of the reaper, then the binder and thresher, transformed agriculture in North America and set the stage for the tremendous growth of Canada and the United States during the latter half of the 19th Century and the first half of the 20th.

But these machines were expensive and complicated—too expensive and complicated for most farmers at first. The separator, in particular, was a machine that was typically only needed for a single day each year, but that cost hundreds or thousands of dollars. As a result, North American farmers developed several schemes to insure that the grain crop would be threshed without each individual farmer having to buy his own machine.

The most common of these schemes was the threshing ring, a group of farmers who formed a kind of partnership or corporation that owned and operated a threshing machine (and sometimes the tractor, steam or gasoline, that powered it). These rings could include as few as two or three farmers or as many as fifteen or more, with acreage totaling just 160 acres **or** up to 1,600 acres or more. Some rings were formed of adjacent farms while others might be scattered across many miles.

The organization and management of these rings became a very important part of most American farmer's operations. Even a small thresher cost about $1,000 during the 1920s, plus several hundred dollars more each season of use. This was a substantial investment and most rings before World War II used written contracts to formalize the roles and responsibilities of each ring member. And besides the simple cost of machine and fuel, sorting out the value of the labor contributed by each-and the benefit to each-can get extremely complicated, another good reason for written agreements.

85

The worst job on the threshing crew goes to the boys and young men working the straw pile—hot, dusty, dirty work.

A 1921 University of Illinois study of threshing labor revealed tremendous differences between the contributions of ring members, even when acreage were similar. One farmer might have a lot of grain to harvest but little labor to contribute, while another might have just a few acres and five or six sturdy lads ready to work. The members of these rings developed sometimes elaborate accounting schemes to equalize the costs and the profits from participation.

This study documented an eight member ring; acreage varied from 25 to 65 and yields from 27 to 46 bushels per acre. When the threshing was complete the data revealed tremendous disparities from one farm to the next—only 741 bushels on one farm, over 4,400 on another. Each member furnished just one or two men, a total of 12. The ring threshed 15,407 bushels of oats during 148 hours of operation—1,284 bushels per man. Obviously, some members of the

ring get a lot more benefit than others-the farmer with 4,400 bushels got much more work out of the thresher and the crew (46 man hours) than did the farmer with just 741 bushels who needed just eight man hours and supplied just one man to the ring.

Bushel-Based Settlement

One way threshing rings evened things up was to calculate a charge for each member's crop based on the numbers of bushels threshed—12 men worked the ring, each averaging 1,284 bushels. Farmer Bob, with his 4,400 bushels, supplied two

Although the canvases for the feeder are new, most of the machine is original. It takes a big tractor or engine to power such a thresher, but when up to speed and with sufficient horsepower, even the clumsiest bunch of bundle-pitchers can't slug it.

A Day of Thanksgiving

My Grandfather, Charles Kubicek, once commented on the genteel, but intense competition for best cook as the threshing ring traveled from farmstead to farmstead. The meals, he affirmed, were hot, a lot and velmy dobre (very good). He also commented that even during Prohibition, the last meal served to the threshing crew on Czech and German farms in the neighborhood included a glass of beer.

Whether it was home brewed, bootleg, or purchased it was a glass of beer served as a special treat and with a certain old world dignity in recognition of the threshing and threshers. Indeed, whether the harvest was good, bad or break-even, the work was hard, the days long, and there was real danger of injury. And, there was also a sense of family, of community and of mutual respect reaffirmed with the completion of the harvest at each farm. To him, that glass of beer represented a chalice of all the values and efforts of farming, of threshing and of threshers.

Terry Kubicek

Yours For Success
Lorraine, Kansas–August 27, 1902

Gentlemen:

I wish to say that the New Century Separator I bought of your agents at Lorraine, Kansas, has given entire satisfaction. I have threshed all kinds of grain, some very weedy and wet, and separated and cleaned it all in first class shape. I have threshed for the last eight years and have run three different makes of machines, but never seen one that could come up to the New Century. The farmers say they don't want any better threshing than I do with it. Your separating and cleaning device is perfect and there is no cylinder that can beat the New Century.

Yours for success,
Richard Peters

men to the ring, the labor of both earning a credit of 2,568 bushels. Since they used the ring to thresh 1,845 bushels more than average, Farmer Bob owed the ring for that amount—calculated at 2.8 cents per bushel in this part of Illinois during the 1920s. Farmer Bob, then, owed the ring $53.14 for his extra threshing.

Farmer Frank's contribution was worth 1,284 bushels but he only needed 741 bushels of work—so his labor earned him a cash credit for the difference of 543 bushels at 2.8 cents each, $15.14.

Acreage-Basis Settlement

Members of threshing rings settled up other ways, too. One was on the basis of the acreage of each member—a system that only works if the yield on each farm is similar to that of the others. In the University of Illinois study yields varied tremendously, from 27 bushels to the acre, to 46! Obviously, the acreage settlement method wouldn't be fair for the farmers of this ring.

Time-Based Settlement

Another method threshing rings applied for equalizing the contributions of the members settled up on the basis of the number of hours each contributed. The 1921 study found that the labor varied tremendously, with one of the eight farmers contributing 46 hours to the effort, while another only put in 13 hours. When the time method was used for settlement, the hours contributed by each ring member for threshing each crop was carefully recorded; if Farmer Bob's crop needed 460 man hours of work and his contribution was just 204 hours, he was charged for the difference—256 hours. The rate in 1921 was 25 cents per hour, or $64 for Farmer Bob. Farmer Frank, though, furnished 140 hours of work and earned a credit of 52 hours—and a check for $13 at the end of the run.

The Small Threshing Ring

The small ring usually had three to six farms and about 160 to 300 acres of grain to thresh. Only six to nine men were required for the crew of such a small operation, and the smallest model thresher would normally be adequate—a machine with a 22 inch by 36 inch cylinder powered by a tractor with about 20 to 30 belt horsepower.

Paul Reno signals "speed up" to the tractor operator from his perch atop a McCormick-Deering thresher during a demonstration at the Koster ranch.

The Large Threshing Ring

A large threshing ring might have 15 or 20 member farmers and 1,600 or more acres of grain to harvest. A project like that would take the biggest thresher on the market, typically a 36x60-inch machine, powered by a 50 or 60 horsepower tractor or steam engine, and crewed by 30 or 40 men and boys. The cost of that big thresher would be double the price of a smaller unit, but it would more than double the output. Managing a ring this size is a major chore, with lots of headaches, responsibilities, and conflicts—plus huge expenses to control. And serving dinner to 40 members of the ancient and honorable Brotherhood of Threshermen would require a whole platoon of cooks and servers and pot scrubbers.

Co-operative Ownership of Threshing Machines

The typical arrangement for rings back before World War II was for each member to contribute the same amount toward the purchase of the new threshing machine. In most rings with a small to moderate sized machine, that meant each had to kick in anywhere from $100 to $400, depending on the size of the group and the cost of the machine. A typical small thresher, though, cost about $1,000 at the time, so each member of even a small ring had the use of the machine at a far lower cost than if he bought it for his exclusive use.

But the ring again had the problem of making things fair for all participants, some who would use the machine more than others. The rings quickly developed ways to settle up fairly for the use of the machine, too, normally by making a charge for each bushel of grain threshed by the machine. If everybody has the same amount of grain threshed no money changes hands. But that's not the way it usually works in practice. So the ring treasurer calculates a charge (2.5 cents per bushel in the study) for each farm, just for use of the machine; one farmer with 8,000 bushels would owe $200 while another with just 2,000 bushels would only owe $50.

Jacob Yoder pitching bundles into the feeder. He and Merlin clean the whole wagon-load of bundles in about ten minutes of steady work, then return for another load. They easily thresh a year's worth of oats in an afternoon.

Cleaned grain flows from the machine in a yellow flood.

Steam Shows Around America

These shows are favorites of some of the author's friends in the hard-core steam fan community, and are just a very few of the huge number of events held to celebrate the heritage of farm heritage around the U.S. The dates can vary considerably, so be sure to consult one of the directories or the show itself for particulars.

- Pioneer Peanut Days, presented by the Dixie Flywheelers Association, Post Office Box 6363, Dothan, Alabama 36302; normally toward the end of October.
- California Antique Farm Show, presented by Early Days Gas Engine & Tractor Club Branch 8, Post Office Box 1475, Tulare, California 93275; normally in late April.
- Semi-Annual Threshing Bee, Antique Tractor & Engine Show, Early Days Gas Engine & Tractor Assn., 2040 North Santa Fe Road, Vista, California 92024; normally in mid-June.
- Connecticut Antique Tractor Show and Pull, Route 169, Brooklyn Fairgrounds, Brooklyn, Connecticut. For info call 1-800-442-5182. Normally held in mid-October.
- Sunbelt Ag Expo, Post Office Box 28, Tifton, Georgia 31793, but held at the fairgrounds at Moultrie in mid-October.
- River Valley Antique Association's Threshing Show and Antique Display, Three Sisters Park south of Chillicothe, Illinois, on Route. 29; Held in late September.
- Fall Festival, Boonville, Indiana, (812) 925-7666; held in mid October.

- Missouri River Valley Steam Engine Assn., Booneville, Missouri; normally in mid-September.
- Thresherman's Reunion, Pontiac, Illinois; Labor Day weekend.
- Rock River Thresheree, Edgerton, Wisconsin; Labor Day weekend.
- Badger Steam and Gas Show, Baraboo, Wisconsin; late August.
- Northwestern Pennsylvania Steam Engine & Old Equipment Assn. Porterville, Pennsylvania.
- Tri-State Steam Show, Findleyville, Pennsylvania.
- Pioneer Steam & Gas Engine Society of NW Pennsylvania, Saegertown, Pennsylvania; late July.
- Midwest Old Threshers, Mt. Pleasant, Iowa, 1887 245th Street, Mt. Pleasant, Iowa 52641 (319) 385-8937; One of the giant shows; Labor Day weekend.
- Michigan Steam Engine and Threshers Club, Mason, Michigan.
- Western Minnesota Steam Threshers Reunion, Rollag, Minnesota; Another giant show—Mecca for the steam traction engine community; Labor Day weekend.
- And a whole lot more can be found in the Antique Power Show Guide, Post Office Box 562, Yellow Springs, Ohio 45387; 1-800-767-5828.
- And also in the StemGas Show Directory, Post Office Box 328, Lancaster, Pennsylvania 17608.

There is a lot of grain in this straw pile, the result of a too much air coming from the cleaning fan. Such problems are common at the beginning of a "set," and adjustments on the machine will quickly fix the problem.

A properly sewn sack is full, rigid, and heavy. Depending on the crop, each weighs about 70 pounds. The sack-sewer makes two handy "ears" to serve as handles to move the sack. During a full day of this, in the old days, a sack-sewer could easily close and carry over a thousand heavy bags—not a job for the weak or lazy.

One of the key members of the harvest crew out west was the "sack sewer," a man whose embroidery might not be very delicate, but was often admired. An average thresher will pump out a full sack every 30 seconds, and that sack must be closed up tight and strong enough to be wrestled onto a wagon. It is a job that requires strength, speed, and skill in pretty much equal measures.

Freshly threshed grain in a bulk grain wagon.

John Slauter, Thresherman

I started working on a thrashing crew in 1938, when I was 14 years old, and continued until 1958, when I bought the first combine in the neighborhood. My father was part of a large threshing ring, about fifteen farmers, although the number varied from year to year. The tractor back then was a big Massey Harris, and I think they used a Case separator, but that varied from year to year, too.

My first job was waterboy, and I carried jugs of water around to the men working out in the field and on the thresher. Actually, the waterboy on the job is accountable to the farmer who's crop is getting threshed—he hired and paid us. One lady was kind of cantankerous—she charged me for each cork I lost from the water jug, and that left me at the end of the day with very little payment for my work! But she was the only one on our ring who was like that because the rest were very gracious and made sure we were fed well and that the little waterboy had what he needed to do his job.

I carried two stoneware jugs on cords, draped across my saddle, and I rode my little pony on my rounds. I had to make sure the men in the field had water, and they wanted it as cool as I could get it, so the jugs were wrapped in wet gunny sacks. It was a job that kept you constantly busy during the whole day. It was hot and the fellers were always thirsty! Most were always real appreciative, but once in a while one might be irritable. Overall, though, the waterboy felt he was contributing to the work in a big way! You had to put up with a lot of "tease and torment" that went along with the job—like the guy who always gave my pony a swat on the rump after he had his drink. But we got to eat with the men and enjoy their fellowship and the little waterboy felt pretty big. The most I ever got paid was a dollar a day, and my dinner! And that is how I started out on the threshing crew!

John Slauter

Ardenwood Historic Farm's Case thresher set up and ready for business. Ardenwood hosts two harvest festivals, one in July, another in October-both well worth attending. Many similar events can be found across Canada and the United States, and in Great Britain as well.

"Spike Scooping"

After being a waterboy, my next advancement was as a driver of a grain wagon, carrying the grain from the thrasher to the granary. I could scoop grain right- or left-handed-somebody who can do that is called a "spike scooper." When they discovered I could do that, my job was at the bin. I unloaded the wagons as they came in, a job I liked because there was always plenty of cool water and there was usually a little breeze and shade up in the barn. It could keep you busy, though, when the crop was good—it didn't take long to fill one of those wagons. And that was my job for the rest of the time I helped on a threshing ring.

Most of the farms in our ring were about 300 acres, with about a third of that in grain. We'd thresh each farm in a day, or day and a half, with the biggest taking two. The owners of those big farms had to supply more labor to the ring to compensate for our extra work, and generally they did. I liked the big places; the food was usually good and I could get two or three excellent threshing dinners at these places—and sometimes an evening meal, too. That was good because we might be threshing until quite late, then have to go home for evening chores. My mother appreciated that, too, because she didn't have to wait till eleven at night when we were finally through with the day to feed us. But the next morning we'd be up early and right back at it.

I didn't get paid for my work once I graduated from the position of waterboy. Then I was helping my dad, providing exchange labor with the other farmers. But we didn't mind that—it was a chance to get away from home, to have some great meals, have some fun, and maybe jump in a pond at the end of the day.

Threshing even helped with my education. I remember one time, after a big noon meal, one of the older men, a bundle wagon driver, introduced us boys to chewing tobacco. That was the sickest I have ever been, and it weaned me from chewing tobacco for life!

John Slauter

It is not unusual for a thresher to need some special attention at the beginning of a "set," particularly when the rig is recently overhauled, as this one is. The "tailings" are closely inspected for clues about what might be happening inside.

PERIODICALS

ADVANCE-RUMELY
The Rumely Newsletter
P.O. Box 12
Moline, IL 61265
309/764-6753

Rumely Collector s News
12109 Mennonite Church Rd.
Tremont, IL 61568
309/925-3932

ALLIS-CHALMERS
Old Allis News
10925 Love Rd.
Bellevue, MI 49021
616/763-9770

The Allis Connection
161 Hillcrest Ct.
Central City, IA 52214
319/438-6234

CASE
J.I Case Collectors Assn.
Old Abe s News
Rt. 2 Box 242
Vinton, OH 45686-9741
614/388-8895

HART-PARR/OLIVER
Oliver Collector s News
RR 1 Box 44
Manvel, ND 58256-0044

FORD
The 9N-2N-8N-NAA Newsletter
154 Blackwood Lane
Stamford, CT 06903
203/322-7283

IHC
Red Power Magazine
Box 277
Battle Creek, IA 51006
712/365-4873 (evenings)

JOHN DEERE
Green Magazine
RR 1
Bee, NE 68314

MASSEY-FERGUSON
Massey Collectors News
Box 529
Denver, IA 50622
319/984-5292

MINNEAPOLIS-MOLINE
M-M Corresponder Magazine
3693 M Avenue
Vail, IA 51465
712/677-2433

The Prairie Gold Rush
RR 1 Box 119
Francesville, IN 47946
219/567-2604

GENERAL INTEREST
Antique Power Magazine
P.O. Box 562
Yellow Springs, OH 45387
800/767-5828

Belt Pulley Magazine
P.O. Box 83
Nokomis, IL 62075
217/563-2612

Engineers and Engines
2240 Oak Leaf St
P.O. Box 2757
Joliet, IL 60434-2757

Dave Cook supervises while the volunteers start feeding bundles.

Farm Antiques News
P.O. Box 812
Tarkio, MO 64491
816/736-4528

Gas Engine Magazine
P.O. Box 328
Lancaster, PA 17608
717/392-0733

The Hook
(antique tractor pulling)
P.O. Box 937
Powell, OH 43065-0937
614/848-5038

Early Day Engine & Tractor Ass n
3510 Brooklake Rd
Brooks, OR 97303
717/392-0733

INDEX